Promising Practices for Family and Community Involvement during High School

A volume in
Family–School–Community Partnership Series
Diana Hiatt-Michael, *Series Editor*

LIST OF CONTRIBUTORS

Jacquelynne S. Eccles
McKeachie Collegiate Professor of Psychology,
Women's Studies, and Education
University of Michigan

Catherine M. Hands
Assistant Professor, Leadership Studies
University of San Diego

Holly Kreider
Vice President, Sociometrics

Joan Lampert
Concordia University, Chicago
Retired Coordinator, Freshman Advisory and Family Center Programs
Maine East High School, Park Ridge, IL

Jack Shelton
Director, PACERS, Incorporated

Lee Shumow
Professor, Leadership, Educational Psychology &
Foundations Department
Northern Illinois University

Hilton Smith
Chair of Secondary Education, Piedmont College
Coordinator of the Foxfire–Piedmont Partnership

Marie-Anne Suizzo
Associate Professor, Educational Psychology
University of Texas at Austin

Nicole Zarrett
Assistant Professor, Department of Psychology
University of South Carolina

Jennifer Dounay Zinth
Senior Policy Analyst, Education Commission of the States

Promising Practices for Family and Community Involvement during High School

edited by

Lee Shumow
Northern Illinois University

INFORMATION AGE PUBLISHING, INC.
Charlotte, NC • www.infoagepub.com

Library of Congress Cataloging-in-Publication Data

Shumow, Lee.
Promising practices for family and community involvement during high school / edited by Lee Shumow.
p. cm. – (Family school community partnership issues)
Includes bibliographical references.
ISBN 978-1-60752-124-2 (pbk.) – ISBN 978-1-60752-125-9 (hardcover)
1. Community and school–United States. 2. High schools–United States. 3. Education, Secondary–Parent participation–United States. I. Shumow, Lee. II. Title.
LC221.S48 2009
373.119–dc22

2009014755

Printed in the United States of America

CONTENTS

SECTION TWO

PERSPECTIVES FROM PRACTICE AND POLICY

ACKNOWLEDGEMENTS

As the Issue Editor of this monograph, I appreciate the assistance and support of all those who helped bring this issue to fruition. Diana Hiatt-Michael, the Series Editor, provided invaluable counsel from start to finish. The Executive Board and members of the Family School Community Partnership SIG of the American Educational Research Association shared their knowledge and endorsed the issue topic, chapter topics, and contributors. Reviewers were drawn from the membership. Their insightful careful reading of particular chapters and their suggestions for improvement were invaluable. I am grateful to the following SIG members for serving as reviewers: Martha Allexsaht-Snider, Jeffrey V. Bennett, Susan Bernstein, Rama Cousik, Nancy Erbstein, Damen Harris, Anne Henderson, Suzannah Hermann, Amy Hilgendorf, Esther Katenga, Revathy Kumar, Margy McClain, Luis Pena, Steven Sheldon, Bricca Sweet, Loizos Symeou, Sally Wade, and Adriane Williams.

I appreciate the authors who contributed a chapter to this monograph. Their names and professional affiliations can be seen in the list of contributors. Each of the authors dedicated a considerable amount of their time to writing these chapters. It was a pleasure to work with them and I thank them for sharing their expertise with us.

I extend my gratitude to my colleagues and to the administrators at Northern Illinois University who support my scholarly endeavors. Finally, I thank my family—my parents, Earl and Rita Bakalars, who were model parents and educators; my husband, Mark, who has always supported my passion for education and scholarship; and my children who allowed me to live the meaning of this book.

Promising Practices for Family and Community Involvement during High School, page vii

FOREWORD

Welcome to the seventh monograph in the Family–School–Community Partnership Series. This series of monographs has been edited and developed by members of the American Educational Research Association's (AERA) Special Interest Group–Family, School, Community Partnerships (SIG-FSCP). This volume is directed towards research to practice issues related to partnering with families of adolescents and the communities in which schools are located in order to promote the success and adjustment of high school students.

Partnering with families is widely accepted, practiced, and researched during the preschool and elementary years. However, only recently, researchers have focused on the benefits of partnerships between families and schools at the secondary school level. This monograph introduces current theory related to the developmental needs of adolescents and their parents; developing trust in partnerships among families, the youth, communities, and school personnel throughout this period of adolescent development; and includes descriptions of stellar programs that meet those needs. Each chapter will assist those who work with adolescents to understand developmental needs of youth, and work with their families and the community to promote strong academic and social outcomes for these youth. Important issues include transition to secondary schooling and reduction of school dropouts, open communication skills among youth, families, and the school community, programs and activities that empower youth, and working with families to promote academic readiness for higher education. This monograph opens new vistas to practitioners at the secondary level as well as researchers in FSCP.

For this monograph, Lee Shumow, Professor of Educational Psychology and Presidential Teaching Professor, at Northern Illinois University accepted

---

Promising Practices for Family and Community Involvement during High School, pages ix–xi the SIG-FSCP invitation to serve as Editor. Shumow, who has been a leading force in family–school–community partnerships for many years, served as the SIG-FSCP's chair from 2001–2003. Under her leadership, these monographs were initiated, supported, and flourished. Shumow closely worked with me throughout the creation of the procedures and practices, laying a strong groundwork for subsequent monograph development.

Her particular credentials that led to the uniqueness of this monograph are that she teaches adolescent development to students who are seeking middle and secondary school teacher certification. She developed a popular course for educators at the graduate level which focuses on using resources from, and forging relationships with, families and the community to improve schools.

Shumow's research and writing connect knowledge of families and community with the academic adjustment of adolescents. Her recent publications that focus on the topic of this monograph include the following:

Father's and mother's school involvement during early adolescence (2001) in *The Journal of Early Adolescence*

Parental efficacy: Predictor of parenting behavior and adolescent outcomes (2002) in *Parenting: Science and Practice*

Family and community as sources of educational adjustment (2003) in *Thresholds in Education*

Adolescents' participation in service activities and its impact on academic, behavioral, and civic outcomes (2007) in *Journal of Youth and Adolescence*

Reading in class and out: An Experience Sampling Method study (2008) in *Middle Grades Research Journal*

Adolescent's experience doing homework: Associations among context, quality of experience, and social–emotional outcomes (2008) in the *School Community Journal*

Family matters: Exploring the complexities of families of immigrants adolescents and achievement in four G8 Countries (2008) in the *Open Family Studies Journal*

Educational outcomes for young adolescents in self care: Moderating effects of family and community characteristics (2009) in the *Journal of Early Adolescence*

Shumow has received numerous awards, in particular three teaching awards at Northern Illinois University, including the *Excellence in Undergraduate Teaching* Award in 2005 and the *Presidential Teaching Award* in 2007.

In addition, she received an American Association of Colleges of Teacher Education Parental Engagement and Partnership grant. For that work she was awarded the *Contributions to School Community Partnerships* recognition award from the College of Education at NIU.

For this monograph, Shumow selected outstanding researchers and program developers in adolescent and family/community education. She organized individuals to serve as a review board for the thrust of this monograph, to select topics of chapters, and as reviewers for the chapters. Thus, I knew that this volume was in kind and skilled hands. My deepest appreciation goes to her for her care and nurturing of the authors and chapters that comprise this timely and important monograph.

The initial monograph entitled *Promising Practices for Family Involvement in Schools* and published in late 2001 synthesized research and practice across the generic elements of family involvement in schooling. The first monograph was followed by annual monographs that addressed various types of family involvement concerns such as: community involvement in *Promising Practices to Connect Schools with the Community*, families of children with special needs in *Promising Practices Connecting Schools to Families of Children with Special Needs*, global concerns in *Promising Practices for Family Involvement Across the Continents*, and families of English language learners in *Promising Practices for Teachers to Engage Families of English Language Learners*. In these monographs we noted that a major body of research attended to elementary school issues.

Thus, the sixth volume titled *Promising Practices for Partnering with Families in the Early Years* addressed family involvement practices across a variety of settings and programs at the early childhood level; and the current volume focuses on adolescents within the interconnecting context of their schools, their families, and their communities. As always, the SIG-FSCP and I are deeply grateful to George Johnson, President, Information Age Publishing, for his support and guidance throughout the years.

Diana B. Hiatt-Michael
Series Editor, Family–School–Community Partnership Series

CHAPTER 1

INTRODUCTION TO PROMISING PRACTICES FOR FAMILY AND COMMUNITY INVOLVEMENT DURING HIGH SCHOOL

This volume focuses on family and community connections with education during the high school years. In this introductory chapter I first enumerate the reasons that the volume is needed. I then describe how the volume is structured, and finish by highlighting the contributions of each chapter to the overall work.

RATIONALE FOR A VOLUME OF FAMILY, SCHOOL, COMMUNITY CONNECTIONS

First, the topic of family, school, and community connections has been relatively neglected as it pertains to high schools by both practitioners and policy makers. In comparison to the wealth of attention that has been focused on involving parents with schools during the early childhood and elementary school years, less attention has been directed to parents of

---

Promising Practices for Family and Community Involvement during High School, pages 1–5

high school students. The development of educational programs to forge connections between family, community, students, and educators at the high school level has lagged far behind programs developed for younger children. Similarly, policymakers have acted more often to encourage and increase family and community involvement with schools when children are young than when they are adolescents. Researchers have described the influences of families and communities on high school students but have studied practices or programs that connect students, families, communities, and schools less often and for a shorter time than they have studied practices in the lower grades, probably because, as noted, practices to involve families are more prevalent during early childhood and the elementary grades.

Second, researchers have found that family and community continue to have a very significant impact on student achievement and on post secondary enrollment and attainment even though parental involvement with schools declines considerably by high school. Some of that decline is due to the structure of high schools, in that teachers typically have many more students than they have in the younger grades (Dornbusch & Glasgow, 1996; Eccles & Harold, 1996), and some is due to the increased difficulty of the curriculum in high school which often precludes most parents from being able to assist directly with school work (Patrikou, 2004; Simon, 2001). Another reason for the decline is related to the misconception that adolescents do not need or want their parents involved and comes at least partly from the fact that adolescents are developing autonomy. Yet, as a parent I recently interviewed said, “They might say they don’t want you but, of course they want you, and are hurt if you don’t show up!” Surveys conducted with adolescents support that statement (Deslandes & Cloutier, 2002). In terms of the community, adolescents have much greater mobility than younger children so they tend to get around their communities more, but their engagement with the community is not likely to foster their academic adjustment unless adults mediate the connections.

A third reason for a volume focusing on the high school is that educators know that family and community factors are important for student success in high school. At the same time, educators identify working with families and connecting the curriculum to the community as difficult. This is not surprising because they face a lack of preparation for collaborating with families and communities (Hiatt-Michaels, 2004). There are also few examples of effective programs for them to follow (Harvard Family Research Project, 2006). This is unfortunate because the more educators solicit parent involvement during high school, the more parents respond (Simon, 2001).

STRUCTURE OF THE VOLUME

The field of family school community partnerships is interdisciplinary. Scholars from the fields of developmental psychology, education, educational leadership, educational policy, sociology, and human services are involved in conducting research to better understand how schools can best enhance the education of the young through interactions with students' families and communities. Educational practitioners also are pioneering efforts to involve and serve families as well as to connect with communities in order to enrich the educational environment and enlarge opportunities for students, teachers, families, and community members. This volume reflects the interdisciplinary nature of the field. The contributors were recruited from diverse fields and workplaces. Chapters are organized into two sections to reflect whether the genesis of the work described is from theory and research or from practice and policy.

Chapter Contributions

Perspectives from Theory and Research

Chapter Two approaches the importance of family involvement with high school students through the lens of adolescent development. Holly Kreider and Marie-Anne Suizzo review the key developmental tasks of adolescence and describe what research says about contributors to and outcomes of family processes that support development and school success among high school students. With an eye on the contemporary landscape, they identify and elaborate on promising strategies that can be used to engage families in their high school student's development in the twenty-first century. As they point out, there is a need for more researchers to examine the potency of these strategies.

Nicole Zarret and Jacquelyn Eccles also take a developmental perspective in examining the complex interacting factors that promote high school students engagement in extracurricular activities. They review the research on how and why adolescents choose to get involved and stay involved in developmentally instigative activities after school. They identify reciprocal processes between student motivation, family and community factors, and the activity context. Their chapter is organized by a theoretical framework that elucidates how practitioners might best promote participation among high school students and how researchers might seek to better understand the processes and outcomes of student participation and practitioner efforts.

In the next chapter, Catherine Hands focuses on the nature and importance of trust in building partnerships. Hands extends the literature on school partnerships by examining trust through the theoretical framework proposed by Bottery. She then exemplifies how varying types of trust play out in the high school partnerships she studied. In this way, her chapter serves as a model of how theory and research can inform practice because school leaders can use the ideas and examples presented in this chapter to plan for new partnerships and reflect upon existing ones.

Perspectives from Practice and Policy

Joan Lampert's work as a practitioner in a high school has been nationally recognized (2005). In her chapter she describes how needs assessment, collaborative team effort, theory, and knowledge from research were utilized to plan programs that assist high school students with the critical issue of transition to high school and to design a program to serve and involve families. Educational leaders, teachers, human service providers, and community agencies can learn from the thorough and effective programs she describes in her chapter. Academics recognize that theory is tested in practice and can look to those programs for examples of applied developmental psychology.

Hilton Smith writes about the highly regarded Foxfire Program. Foxfire arose from the need of a teacher to engage his students. A key to that program and what it has become was the realization that the communities high school students lived in could serve as the text they studied, the impetus for developing a sense of agency in the young, and the vehicle for belonging to something beyond a traditional high school class. Smith uses anecdotes from his own practice as a high school teacher and from other high school teachers to show how high school students and teachers learn from and contribute to their communities and he acknowledges the difficulties encountered in truly "walking the walk" that Dewey championed. His chapter provides examples of what educators might accomplish by working with students to learn from and contribute to their communities and as a challenge for researchers who need to do more to study this enduring educational program.

Jack Shelton has been a pioneer in terms of establishing high school partnerships with businesses and in communities. Like the Foxfire Program, PACERS engages students in doing work that matters in their communities. The opportunities for career and identity development provided by PACERS are exemplary. Educators will find specific guidance about key factors in implementing such programs. Researchers may find ideas about how to test theory in practice and be motivated to design and study similar innovative programs.

Jennifer Dounay, a policy analyst, contributed the final chapter on state policies that support parental involvement in adolescents' postsecondary plans. This is a crucial topic because the vast majority of contemporary high school students need a postsecondary education in order to prepare them for the types of jobs that can sustain a middle class(or higher) lifestyle. She provides examples of what states have done to promote effective practices in high schools.

REFERENCES

Deslandes, R., & Cloutier, R. (2002). Adolescents' Perception of Parental Involvement in Schooling. *School Psychology International, 23*(2), 220–232

Dornbush, S. & Glasgow, K. (1996). The structural context of family–school relations. In A. Booth & J. Dunn (Eds.), *Family–school links: How do they affect educational outcomes* (pp. 35–44). Mahwah, NJ: Erlbaum.

Eccles, J. & Harold, R. (1996). Family involvement in children's and adolescents' school. In A. Booth & J. Dunn (Eds.), *Family–school links: How do they affect educational outcomes* (pp. 3–34). Mahwah, NJ: Erlbaum.

Harvard Family Research Project (2006). Challenges and opportunities in moving family involvement research into practice. Presentation at Family–School Relations during Adolescence: linking Interdisciplinary Research and Practice, Durham NC: Duke University Sanford Institute of Public Policy. Retrieved November 16, 2008, from http://www.hfrp.org/family-involvement/publications-resources/challenges-and-opportunities-in-moving-family-involvement-research-into-practice-presentation.

Hiatt-Michaels, D. (2004). Preparing teachers or parental involvement: Current practices and possibilities across the nation. *Thresholds in Education, 30*(2), 2–10.

Lampert, J. (2005). Easing the transition to high school. *Educational Leadership, 62*(7), 61–63.

Patrikakou, E. (2004). Adolescence: Are parents relevant to students' high school achievement and post-secondary attainment. *Family Involvement Research Digest.* Cambridge, MA: Harvard Family Research Project. Retrieved November 16, 2008, from http://www.hfrp.org/family-involvement/publications-resources/adolescence-are-parents-relevant-to-students-high-school-achievement-and-post-secondary-attainment.

Simon, B. (2001). Family involvement in high school: Predictors and effects. *NASSP Bulletin, 85*(627), 8–19.

SECTION ONE

PERSPECTIVES FROM THEORY AND RESEARCH

CHAPTER 2

ADOLESCENT DEVELOPMENT AND FAMILY INVOLVEMENT

Holly Kreider and Marie-Anne Suizzo

Why consider and even encourage family involvement in the lives of adolescents, when adolescents themselves may want nothing more than to be left alone or in the company of their friends? First, adolescents do want to maintain connections to their parents and other adult caregivers (Deslandes & Cloutier, 2002), albeit in different ways than younger children do. Second, adolescence is often considered a watershed period in development, characterized by dramatic physical changes, powerful peer influences, and risk-taking behaviors (Steinberg & Morris, 2001). However, most youth pass through this period unscathed, often because their parents and other caregivers continue to exert considerable influence in their lives. Third, there is wide agreement that family involvement in children's learning benefits children's socioemotional and cognitive/academic outcomes (Henderson & Mapp, 2002). Although much research has focused on family involvement in early and middle childhood, evidence of its benefits during adolescence is also compelling (Kreider, Caspe, Kennedy & Weiss, 2007). Yet family involvement tends to decline during and even before children reach middle school, and declines further as students reach high school (Spera, 2005). Researchers speculate that increasingly complex school structures,

Promising Practices for Family and Community Involvement during High School, pages 9–25

students' heightened desire for autonomy, and parents' waning knowledge of subject matter may explain this decline (Eccles & Harold, 1993). By shining a spotlight on family involvement during adolescence, we hope to bring into sharp relief its importance during this developmental period, as well as ways to connect the research to educational practice.

Examining family involvement in adolescence has special significance at this point in history. The face of youth today continues to shift—with racial and ethnic diversity increasing rapidly and projected to increase even more in coming decades (Forum on Child and Family Statistics, 2007). Globalization also has created an increasingly competitive environment for young adults entering the workplace and a resultant pressure on schools and families to prepare students well for these realities. Today's youth also face new risks and environments unknown to earlier generations like high rates of HIV infection and the explosion of technology-based communications and social networking websites like MySpace.

In this chapter, we consider family involvement in children's learning during this critical developmental period and at this point in history. We begin by examining key developmental tasks of adolescence, then consider family involvement processes during this period, as well as what facilitates its occurrence, and the positive outcomes it can lead to. Finally, we discuss promising strategies for engaging families in their youth's development. We define family involvement broadly, as any activity parents and other primary caregivers engage in to support their adolescent's learning. We focus intentionally on middle adolescence, roughly ages 15–18, aligning with the high school focus of this book.

DEVELOPMENTAL TASKS OF ADOLESCENCE

During adolescence, children's reasoning ability becomes increasingly complex (Moshman, 1998). This cognitive complexity is visible in logical reasoning about abstract representations of objects, events, and people (Piaget, 1983), and in the ability to take others' perspectives when thinking about situations and events (Selman, 1980). Researchers also have shown that working memory continues to increase throughout adolescence (Case, 1998) and that adolescents become more efficient at problem solving (Siegler, 1996). These cognitive advances affect how youth perceive and think about their interactions with family and peers. Because they understand the complexity of abstract principles such as fairness, justice, and loyalty (Turiel, 1998), they begin to question situations and others' demands, which can pose potential conflicts with parents.

Achieving Academically

Recent educational psychology theories suggest that adolescents' motivation to achieve is influenced by a complex constellation of factors. Eccles and Wigfield (2002) proposed Expectancy–Value theory to explain relations between children's academic beliefs, their parents' goals and behaviors with them, and their actual achievement behaviors. Academic beliefs include personal goals, perceptions of their own competence, causal attributions about why they succeed or fail at learning tasks, and judgments about the value of those tasks (Eccles & Wigfield, 2002). These academic beliefs develop and become more complex in adolescence. For example, by age 12, children can distinguish between effort and ability as contributing to their academic success (Nicholls & Miller, 1984), and view ability as a fixed entity that, unlike effort, cannot be increased when needed. Consistently attributing failure to lack of ability may therefore lead to lower self-concept and lower achievement. And as they progress through middle and high school, adolescents increasingly compare their achievements with their peers, which may cause their self-competence beliefs and achievement values to decline further (Wigfield & Eccles, 2002). Parents and families can positively influence their teenagers' self-competence and achievement beliefs and behaviors, as discussed in a later section.

Peer Relations

During adolescence, children's social networks and time spent with peers expand dramatically (Larsen, Richards, Moneta, Holmbeck, & Duckett, 1996). Developing close and supportive peer relationships is considered an essential task of adolescence (Simpson & Roehlkepartain, 2003). These relationships can take the form of friendships, romantic relationships, and cliques or small groups of peers, and provide opportunities to hone social skills and competence, develop intimacy, and experience support (Collins & Steinberg, in press).

Popular belief points to peer pressure as the culprit for risk-taking behaviors common in adolescence, although admiration and emulation of peers, rather than pressure exerted by peers, influence teen behavior more often (Brown, 2004). Although peers influence teens' orientation to youth culture, parents hold more sway with weightier and longer-term issues like moral values and career choices (Smetana, Campione-Barr, & Metzger, 2006). Parents can also influence teens' selection of friends and romantic relationships (Gray & Steinberg, 1999; Mounts, 2001, 2004). The best adjusted adolescents are in fact ones that are highly connected to peers as well as families (Anderson, Sabatelli, & Kosutic, 2007). We explore these latter relationships in a later section.

Solidifying a Sense of Identity

Developing a coherent and complex understanding of one's self and one's identity is another important task of adolescence (Erikson, 1963). To develop this understanding, adolescents ask themselves questions about who they are and what they want across multiple domains of identity choices, including political, moral, religious, gender, ethnic/racial, and career choices. Spending more time with their peers and less time under the supervision of adults, adolescents become aware of local cultural norms and peer expectations for how they should behave in these social relationships. They often face conflicting demands from peers and authority figures, and may be confused and distressed sorting through these choices and their own sense of self. Marcia (1980) proposed that adolescents' identity development can be characterized by four statuses. *Diffusion* is a state during which there is no reflection on one's identity choices, while *achievement* describes a state during which a firm commitment to one's identity is made. *Moratorium* involves intense searching and questioning. *Foreclosure* entails committing to an identity associated with one's family without having questioned it.

For ethnic minority youth, scholars such as Phinney (1993; 1996) argue that cultural identity development occurs in several stages, mirroring the broader identity development theories of Erikson (1963) and Marcia (1980) above. By early adolescence, these youth are clearly aware of their ethnic group membership and its distinct qualities as well as the stereotypes associated with their group. Some adolescents may have a *foreclosed* ethnic identity, accepting the views of their parents and others, while in the *moratorium* stage, they actively question and explore their ethnic identity. As they emerge from this period of exploration and resolve its associated conflicts and contradictions, they are said to have an *achieved* ethnic identity. Researchers have delineated how this process varies for each ethnic group (Cross, 1995; Helms, 1995; Sue, Mak & Sue, 1998).

Parents are critical in facilitating their children's identity development by allowing them the freedom to explore, providing consistent emotional support, and being willing to engage in difficult discussions with respect and understanding (Grotevant & Cooper, 1986). In ethnic minority families, parents sometimes engage in *racial* or *ethnic socialization*, which includes teaching children about their particular cultural or ethnic group, preparing them to face discrimination, and teaching them to be proud of their ethnicity and its heritage (Hughes & Chen, 1997). Recent studies of racial socialization among African American adolescents have identified positive outcomes such as higher self-esteem and self-worth (Tatum, 2004), academic achievement (Murry & Brody, 2002), and racial coping and competence (Johnson, 2001). Some studies suggest that many African American parents continue to impact their children's development during adolescence (Bowman & Howard, 1985), yet little is known about this process among other ethnic minority groups.

FAMILY INVOLVEMENT IN ADOLESCENTS' SCHOOLING

A growing body of research on family educational involvement during adolescence sheds light on its nature, its predictors and positive outcomes, and the significance of families, other learning contexts, and their interconnections.

Family Involvement Processes and Outcomes

In a recent review, Kreider and colleagues reviewed studies linking family involvement to middle and high school students' academic and social outcomes. They identified three family involvement processes: *parenting*, including attitudes, values, and practices; *home–school relationships*, and *responsibility for learning outcomes*, or activities at home and in the community that promote social and academic growth. These processes have been linked with higher grades and test scores, higher self-esteem and social competence, reduced substance abuse, and aspirations for and enrollment in college (Kreider et al., 2007).

Parenting

Parents support their adolescents' academic success through their relationship with their child, their parenting style, and the amount of monitoring they provide. A positive parent–child relationship can temper what parents typically view as the most challenging stage of parenting (Buchanan et al., 2006), one marked by less time spent together, increased conflict, and slightly decreased closeness compared to earlier stages. However, these changes are normative, temporary, and potentially important to fostering adolescents' growing sense of independence (Smetana et al., 2006). Other developmental psychologists point to the interdependence and continued connections with parents and other adults as overlooked but salient processes of adolescence (Gilligan, Lyons & Hamner, 1990). Several parental strategies may support this balance between autonomy and connection. Parental monitoring, or the awareness and tracking of adolescents' activities, peer relations, and whereabouts, permits greater autonomy among youth and leads to their higher achievement, better adjustment, and less delinquency and aggression (Wright & Fitzpatrick, 2006).

Joint-decision making between parents and children during middle adolescence is also associated with better adjustment later on. Among European Americans, an authoritative parenting style (high on both responsiveness and demandingness) generally leads to more psychosocial competence in teens (Steinberg, 2001). Overall, family interactions that allow adolescents the opportunity to express independent thoughts and feelings while maintaining closeness and connection to parents facilitate better outcomes. Efforts to engage parents in their adolescents' schooling during this developmental period must strive for just these types of balanced interactions. Parental styles vary across ethnic and SES groups, and are associated with different outcomes for each group. Authoritarian style has been shown to lead to negative outcomes for European American children. For African American children, however, research is limited and inconclusive. Some research suggests that the strictness component of authoritarian parenting may protect and prepare African American children to face the effects of racial discrimination (Hill & Bush, 2001; Levanthal & Brooks-Gunn, 2003). However, maternal warmth is also an essential component of African American parenting that has been shown to lead to positive outcomes, especially in at-risk youth (Cleveland, Gibbons, Gerrard, Pomery, & Brody, 2005). Chinese American parenting contains aspects of both authoritarian and authoritative styles, emphasizing high involvement and control, as well as high warmth (Chao, 2000).

Home–School Relationships

Aspects of *home–school relationships* that lead to positive adolescent outcomes include communication with teachers, attendance at school events, volunteering and participating in PTOs and leadership groups, as well as college outreach programs. Such relationships provide opportunities for parents to gather information about their adolescents, convey their positive educational values to teachers and students, and learn how to support their child's college preparation and application process (Kreider et al., 2007).

Promoting Learning Outcomes

Finally, parents share responsibility for adolescents' learning outcomes through a process of *academic socialization*, which includes practices such as monitoring school progress, providing stimulating activities, and holding high but reasonable expectations for academic success (Taylor, Clayton, & Rowley, 2004). When parents promote their children's autonomy rather than exert control, they achieve at higher levels (Ng, Kenney-Benson, & Pomerantz, 2004), and show greater interest and enjoyment in learning (Gurland & Grolnick, 2005). Parental monitoring of school progress and talking about the importance of education are associated with greater interest in school (Wentzel, 1998), higher self-efficacy and personal control, and higher actual achievement (Grolnick & Slowiaczek, 1994). Due to a lack of research among Mexican Americans and African Americans, however, we know little about how these relations operate in these groups (Graham & Taylor, 2002).

To address this gap, researchers are designing measures of academic socialization that take account of both explicit behaviors and educationally supportive beliefs and attitudes conveyed in implicit ways to adolescents. Families convey implicit messages to children through stories and lessons about the importance of hard work and education (Suizzo, Robinson, & Pahlke, 2008). For example, Suizzo and Soon (2006) investigated African American, Asian American, Latino, and European American college students' reports of their parents' academic socialization during middle and high school. The authors identified three dimensions: *Emotional autonomy support, demanding hard work*, and *active involvement*. Although all four ethnic groups reported using emotional autonomy support the most, this practice was associated with an internal locus of control only among Asian and European Americans. This finding provides some evidence that parental socialization practices operate differentially on psychological outcomes for adolescents in different ethnic groups, extending our knowledge of how culture shapes parenting and parent–child relationships.

Promoting Family Involvement in Adolescence

What supports these family involvement processes in adolescence? School outreach is one important predictor. Using a large national dataset, Simon found that high school outreach predicted parents' involvement in parenting, volunteering, and learning at home activities. For example, high school staff contact with parents about teens' academic programs, course selections, and plans after high school, positively predicted parents' level of conversation with their teens about school. Despite these findings, most college preparation programs still do not contain a family involvement component, leaving much to be done in this area (Tierney, 2002).

Likewise, contact about teens' plans after high school predicted parents' levels of attendance at postsecondary planning workshops and frequency of communication with their teens about college. Also, providing parents information about how to help teens study positively predicted levels of parent help with teens' homework (Simon, 2004). In other words, information and outreach by schools on specific aspects of adolescents' schooling was associated with increased family involvement in those same domains of learning.

In general, parents of adolescents appear to become involved when they believe that teachers and students expect or desire their involvement. Specifically, perceptions of invitations from teachers predict school involvement for parents of adolescence, while perceptions of student invitations predict involvement of parents at home (Deslandes & Bertrand, 2005). In sum, not just parents, but also teachers and other school staff, as well as students themselves, need to be on board to realize the full potential of family involvement in the adolescent years.

Examples of programs addressing the family involvement processes above abound, although fewer target adolescents. Programs aimed at promoting positive parenting and strong families are plentiful and are often evidence-based (Caspe & Lopez, 2006). For example, the Strengthening Families Program (SFP; www.strengtheningfamiliesprogram.org) offers 16 sessions to at-risk families, with both parents and youth involved, focusing on children's social skills, parenting skills, and family functioning. Evaluation findings suggest that SFP reduces problem behaviors in children; improves school performance; and reduces delinquency, alcohol, and drug use in youth. It has also been successfully adapted and evaluated with diverse cultural groups, including African American, Hispanic, Asian American, Pacific Islander, and Native American families (Kumpfer & Alvarado, 1995).

The evaluation knowledge base about family involvement programs is less strong. A meta-analysis by Mattingly and colleagues found insufficient evidence to conclude that such programs generally have positive impact on children and youth (Mattingly, Prislin, McKenzie, Rodriguez & Kayzar, 2002). However, a core set of positively evaluated program models do exist (for examples see Lopez & Kreider, 2003). For instance, the Parent Institute for Quality Education (PIQE, 2008) provides parents of children, including those in high school, with educational sessions led by credentialed teachers. Sessions cover academic and involvement topics of relevance to parents, especially those new to the U.S., such as home–school collaboration, college preparation, and the U.S. school system. Evaluation studies have shown that PIQE leads to greater parental engagement, as well as greater school persistence, reduced drop out rates, and higher college participation among students (Vidano & Sahafi, 2004).

As a whole, effective family involvement practices involve meeting youth where they are developmentally—by honing in on academic issues and college preparation, tracking and influencing peer relations, participating in school in ways that still give teens needed space apart from their parents, and supporting youth cultural identity development.

PROMISING INVOLVEMENT STRATEGIES

As illustrated above, family involvement in adolescents' learning can take many forms, some more common than others. Below we look beyond the usual suspects to involvement strategies that have gained prominence in recent years, speak to issues of relevance in the twenty-first century, and hold promise for engaging families during their children's adolescence.

Culturally Relevant Programs

Promoting family involvement among cultural/ethnic minority and low-income families can be challenging. Low-income families are more likely to be single-headed households, reducing the time available to parents for communicating with schools and providing extra help or support that may be needed. Even in dual-earner households, low-income parents often hold jobs with little flexibility to take an hour off to visit their child's school for example (Heymann & Earle, 2000). English language learners may also find it challenging to interact with school staff who do not speak their language and are unfamiliar with their cultural beliefs. Parents with low levels of formal education may not be comfortable visiting their children's schools—having had negative experiences at school when they were children or simply being less familiar with school environments, especially if they attended school in another country. They may also feel they have little to offer an academic institution. Inversely, the traditional view of family involvement has focused on translating the culture of schools within the culture of homes (Lopez, Scribner, & Mahitivanichcha, 2001), and has assumed that parent absence in schools signifies their lack of interest in their children's schooling. This "deficit" perspective (Valencia, 1997) is beginning to be reversed, however much more work must be done to build meaningful relationships between families and schools (Valdez, 1996).

Programs aimed at promoting greater family involvement among these groups therefore have very specific aims, including reducing the psychological distance between parents and educators in order to increase parents' comfort with, and involvement in, their children's schooling. This may be accomplished by teachers asking parents about their life experiences and cultural background, respecting their "funds of knowledge," and even asking parents to share this knowledge with students in the classroom (González, Moll, & Tenery, 2005). Teacher home visits are also suggested in order to meet with families, in their own comfortable environment, and to offer those who request it suggestions for how they can support their children's learning.

One culturally and socioeconomically sensitive family involvement program is the "GREAT Families Program" (Smith, Gorman-Smith, Quinn, & Rabiner, 2004), which targets youth who are at risk for aggression and violence. The intervention includes 15 weekly multiple-family meetings during which six aims are addressed: (a) promoting home-school partnerships, (b) enhancing parental monitoring, (c) promoting care and respect through discipline and rules, (d) increasing parent and child coping and management skills, (e) developing healthy, respectful, and effective family communication and problem solving skills, and (f) planning for the future (Smith et al., 2004). This program caters to low-income families by providing transportation to their sessions, on-site childcare for younger children, dinner for the whole family, and financial compensation. In addition, whenever possible, session leaders are matched by ethnicity with the families they are addressing. Program leaders undergo training that includes increasing their knowledge and understanding of cultural differences in family functioning and parental beliefs, such as variations in the effectiveness of various parenting styles by ethnic group. Although relatively new, this program is promising in that it attends to the specific issues faced by low-income and ethnic minority group families.

Technology

Technology holds special significance for youth today, both as a subject to master and as a means through which to communicate. Both of these technology-related activities pose interesting and developmentally-sensitive opportunities for engaging families in adolescents' learning. First consider the increasing attention given to technological literacy in the high school curriculum. Some of these efforts have engaged families by co-teaching youth and parents together. Although it represents a slightly younger adolescent period, consider a group of sixth grade teachers, students, and parents in Athens, Greece who collectively selected information technology as a focus for strengthening home—school partnerships, partly because students had an advantage in understanding the relevant concepts and could take a leadership role in the project. Parents were paired with children other than their own to learn about technology; which proved critical as students later expressed a preference for interacting with their parents at school only when they (the students) requested it, around fun and engaging, as well as academic, activities (Mylonakou & Kekes, 2005). In this way, the project successfully brought parents and students together to learn and interact, while simultaneously respecting students' desire for leadership opportunities and certain forms of autonomy from their own parents, a desire that only increases as students move into middle adolescence.

Technology is also an increasingly prevalent mechanism for communication among youth and between the adults who nurture and teach them. Bouffard (2006) found an encouraging prevalence and positive academic outcomes from internet-based communication (i.e., websites and emails) between parents and their children's high schools. Using data from the Educational Longitudinal Study 2002, she found that 37% of parents of tenth graders report using internet-based communication with schools and that students whose parents use the internet for such purposes have higher math test scores and expectations for educational attainment two years later. Parent–teacher and home–school communication via email, voicemail, and websites may be developmentally advantageous in adolescence. Parents can still monitor their students' academic progress and even peer relations, an especially important parental activity for youth academic and social outcomes (Kreider et al., 2007), while still maintaining a comfortable physical distance from their increasingly independent teens' classroom space. Email may also offer an efficient mode of communication for parents whose children have six or more teachers in secondary school compared to one or two teachers in earlier grades. Researchers suspect that this structural difference in secondary schools partially explains the decline in family involvement as children get older (Eccles & Harold, 1993). In sum, although more research is needed, learning about and communicating through technology may bring youth and parents as well as parents and teachers together in new and developmentally fitting ways, for instance letting parents monitor academics without intrusion.

Sexual Health Education

Physical sexual maturation is a hallmark of adolescence. Risk-taking and experimentation are common in adolescence, and for some this includes risky sexual behaviors. Unfortunately, after more than a decade of decline, national rates of adolescent pregnancy are on the rise again (Harris, 2007). Recent estimates also suggest that 15 to 24 year olds account for nearly half of all new sexually transmitted infections (STIs) and 40% of new HIV infections (Kaiser Family Foundation, 2007). Effective pregnancy and STI/HIV prevention programs often target high schools as a venue for delivery (Card, Lessard & Benner, 2007). Research also points to family involvement as a best practice for preventing teen pregnancy (UC ANR Latino/a Teen Pregnancy Prevention Workgroup, 2004). Specifically, teens are more likely to avoid risky sexual behaviors when they feel supported by and connected to their parents, when their parents monitor and supervise them appropriately, and under some circumstances, when parents communicate to their children their beliefs and values about sex, condoms, and other contraception (Kirby & Ryan, 2005).

Efforts to integrate research-based family engagement practices in adolescent sexual health education programs are afoot, such as a new project funded by the David and Lucile Packard Foundation to engage families and youth in best-practice adolescent pregnancy prevention efforts in Santa Clara County, CA (Sociometrics Corporation, 2008). Likewise, many prevention programs shown to be effective feature parent–child communication as a central component (Card et al., 2007). All of these are school–based, comprehensive programs using group discussion or role play as a means to strengthen parent–child or family/friend communication. Such effective programs and associated activities share developmental features: they target risky sexual behaviors common in adolescence and the multiple contexts of home, peer, and school culture shaping these behaviors, for example by leveraging the power of the peer context in adolescence via group discussions in school-based programs. As Steinberg points out, changing the contexts of risky behaviors may be more powerful than changing the behaviors themselves among adolescents, who often continue to take risks despite knowledge of the consequences (Steinberg & Morris, 2001). These activities also create a parent–free space to discuss issues of concern, yet make parent communication a topic of consideration.

CONCLUSION

Together, this set of promising practices illuminates several important considerations for engaging families in their adolescents' learning. First, educators and researchers must consider family involvement within topical areas of interest and importance to teenagers, from college preparation to technology literacy to sexuality. Likewise, effective and engaging mechanisms for involving youth and families must be exploited and further explored, such as peer group discussion and role play and technology-based home–school communication. Most importantly, family involvement in adolescents' learning shapes and is shaped by the developmental tasks associated with this period, including school success, cultural identity, peer relations, and parental connections that respect youth desire for autonomy.

REFERENCES

Anderson, S. A., Sabatelli, R. M., & Kosutic, I. (2007). Families, urban neighborhood youth centers, and peers as contexts for development. *Family relations, 56,* 346–357.

Bouffard, S. (2006, April). *"Virtual" parent involvement: The role of the internet in parent–school communication.* Paper presented at the annual meeting of the American Educational Research Association, San Francisco, CA.

Bowman, P. J., & Howard, C. (1985). Race-related socialization, motivation, and academic achievement: A study of black youths in three-generation families. *Journal of the American Academy of Child Psychiatry, 24,* 134–141.

Brown, B. B. (2004). Adolescents' relationships with peers. In R. Lerner & L. Steinberg (Eds.), *Handbook of adolescent psychology* (pp. 363–394). Hoboken, NJ: Wiley.

Buchanan, C. M., Eccles, J. S., Flanagan, C., Midgely, C., Feldlaufer, H., & Harold, R. D. (1990). Parents' and teachers' beliefs about adolescents: Effects of sex and experience. *Journal of Youth and Adolescence, 19,* 363– 94.

Card, J. J., Lessard, L., & Benner, T. (2007). PASHA: Facilitating the replication and use of effective adolescent pregnancy and STI/HIV prevention programs. *Journal of Adolescent Health, 40,* 1–14.

Case, R. (1998). The development of conceptual structures. In D. Kuhn & R. S. Siegler (Eds.), *Handbook of child psychology (5th Ed.)Vol 2: Cognition, perception, and language* (pp. 745–800). New York: Wiley.

Caspe, M., & Lopez, M. E. (2006). Lessons from family-strengthening interventions: Learning from evidence-based practice. Harvard Family Research Project, Cambridge, MA.

Centers for Disease Control (2006). STD Surveillance 2006: Special focus profiles: Adolescents and young adults. Retrieved on 1/23/08 at: http://www.cdc.gov/std/stats/adol.htm#ref1

Chao, R. K. (2000). Cultural explanations for the role of parenting in the school success of Asian American children. In R. D. Taylor, & M. C. Wang (Eds.), *Resilience across contexts: Family, work, culture, and community* (pp. 333–363). Mahwah, NJ: Erlbaum.

Cleveland, M. J., Gibbons, F. X., Gerrard, M., Pomery, E. A., & Brody, G. H. (2005). The impact of parenting on risk cognitions and risk behavior: A study of mediation and moderation in a panel of African American adolescents. *Child Development, 76*(4), 900–916.

Collins, W. A., & Steinberg, L. (in press). Adolescent development in interpersonal context. In W. Damon & Lerner, R. (Eds.), *Developmental Psychology: An advanced course.* Hoboken, NJ: Wiley.

Cross, W. E. J. (1995). The psychology of nigrescence: Revising the Cross model. In J. G. Ponterotto, J. M. Casas, L. A. Suzuki, & C. M. Alexander (Eds.) *Handbook of multicultural counseling* (pp. 93–122). Thousand Oaks: Sage.

Deslandes, R., & Bertrand, R. (2005). Motivation of parent involvement in secondary-level schooling. *The Journal of Educational Research, 98,* 164–175.

Deslandes, R., & Cloutier, R. (2002). *Adolescents' perception of parental involvement in schooling.* Thousand Oaks: Sage.

Eccles, J., & Harold, (1993). Parent–school involvement during the early adolescent years. *Teachers College Record, 94,* 568–587.

Eccles, J. S., & Wigfield, A. (2002). Motivational beliefs, values, and goals. *Annual Review of Psychology, 53,* 109–132.

Erikson, E. H. (1963). *Childhood and Society* (2nd Ed.). New York: W. W. Norton.

Forum on Child and Family Statistics (2007). America's Children: Key National Indicators of Well-Being, 2007: Demographic background. Retrieved on 1/31/08 at: http://www.childstats.gov/americaschildren/highlights2.asp

Gilligan, C., Lyons, N.P., & Hamner, T.J. (Eds.) (1990). *Making connections: The relational worlds of adolescent girls at Emma Willard School.* Cambridge, MA: Harvard Press.

González, N., Moll, L., & Tenery, M. F. (2005). Funds of Knowledge for Teaching in Latino Households. In N. González, L. C. Moll, & C. Amanti (Eds.), *Funds of knowledge: Theorizing practices in households, communities, and classrooms* (pp. 89–111). Mahwah, NJ: Erlbaum.

Graham, S., & Taylor, A. Z. (2002). Ethnicity, gender, and the development of achievement values. In A. Wigfield & J. S. Eccles (Eds.). *Development of achievement motivation* (pp. 121–146). San Diego: Academic Press.

Gray, R. B., & Steinberg, L. (1999). Adolescent romance and the parent–child relationship: A contextual perspective. In W. Furman, B.B. Brown & C. Feiring (Eds.), *Contemporary perspectives on adolescent relationships* (pp. 235–265). New York: Cambridge Press.

Grolnick, W. S., & Slowiaczek, M. L. (1994). Parents' involvement in children's schooling: A multidimensional conceptualization and motivation model. *Child Development, 65,* 237–252.

Grotevant, H. D., & Cooper, C. R. (1986). Individuation in family relationships. A perspective on individual differences in the development of identity and role-taking skill in adolescence. *Human Development, 29,* 82–100.

Gurland, S. T., & Grolnick, W. S. (2005). Perceived threat, controlling parenting, and children's achievement orientations. *Motivation and Emotion, 29,* 103–121.

Harris, G. (2007, Dec. 5). Teen birth rates on the rise for first time since '91. *New York Times.*

Helms, J. E. (1995). An update of Helm's White and people of color racial identity models. In J. G. Ponterotto, J. M. Casas, L. A. Suzuki, & C. M. Alexander (Eds.) *Handbook of multicultural counseling* (pp. 181–192). Thousand Oaks: Sage

Henderson, A,. & Mapp, K. (2002). *A new wave of evidence.* Austin, TX: Southwest Education Development Laboratory.

Heymann, S. J., & Earle, A. (2000). Low-income parents: How do working conditions affect their opportunity to help school-age children at risk? *American Educational Research Journal, 37,* 833–848.

Hill, N. E,. & Bush, K. R. (2001). Relationships between parenting environment and children's mental health among African American and European American mothers and children. *Journal of Marriage and Family, 63,* 954–966.

Hughes, D., & Chen, L. (1997). When and what parents tell children about race: An examination of race-related socialization among African American families. *Applied Developmental Science, 1,* 200–214.

Johnson, D. (2001). Parental characteristics, racial stress, and racial socialization processes as predictors of racial coping in middle childhood. In A. M. Neal-Barnett, J. M. Contreras, & K. A. Kerns (Eds.), *Forging links: African American children clinical developmental perspectives* (pp. 57–74). Westport: Prager.

Kaiser Family Foundation (2007). The global HIV/AIDS Epidemic: HIV/AIDS Policy Fact Sheet. Retrieved on 1/23/08 at: http://kff.org/hivaids/upload/3030-103.pdf

Kirby, D., & Ryan, J. (2005). *Sexual risk and protective factors.* Scotts Valley, CA: ETR Associates.

Kreider, H., Caspe, M., Kennedy, S. & Weiss, H. (2007). *Family involvement in middle and high school students' education.* Cambridge, MA: Harvard Family Research Project.

Kumpfer, K. L., & Alvarado, R. (1995). Strengthening families to prevent drug use in multi-ethnic youth. In G. Botvin, S, Schinke, & M. Orlande (Eds), *Drug abuse prevention with multi-ethnic youth* (pp 255–294). Thousand Oaks: Sage.

Larson, R. W., Richards, M. H., Moneta, G., Holmbeck, G., & Duckett, E. (1996). Changes in adolescents's daily interactions with their families from ages 10–18: Disengagement and transformation, *Developmental Psychology, 32,* 744–754.

Levanthal, T., & Brooks-Gunn, J. (2003). Children and youth in neighborhood contexts. *Current Directions in Psychological Science, 12,* 27–31.

López, G. R., Scribner, J. D., & Mahitivanichcha, K. (2001). Redefining parental involvement: Lessons from high-performing migrant-impacted schools. *American Educational Research Journal, 38,* 253–288.

Lopez, M. E. & Kreider, H. (2003). Achieving authentic participation in school reform. *Evaluation Exchange, IV*(2).

Marcia, J. E. (1980). Identity in adolescence. In J. Adelson (Ed.) *Handbook of adolescent psychology.* New York: Wiley.

Mattingly, D. J., Prislin, R., McKenzie, T. L., Rodriguez, J. L., & Kayzar, B. (2002). Evaluating evaluations: The case of parent involvement programs. *Review of Educational Research, 72,* 549–576.

Moshman, D. (1998). Cognitive development beyond childhood. In D. Kuhn & R. S. Siegler (Eds.), *Handbook of child psychology (5th Ed.), Vol. 2: Cognition, Perception, and Language.* (pp. 947–978). New York: Wiley.

Mounts, N. S. (2001). Young adolescents' perceptions of parental management of peer relationships. *Journal of Early Adolescence, 21,* 91–122.

Mounts, N.S. (2004). Adolescents' perceptions of parental management of peer relationships in an ethnically diverse sample. *Journal of Adolescent Research, 19,* 446–467.

Murry, V. M., & Brody, G. H. (2002). Racial socialization processes in single-mother families: Linking maternal racial identity, parenting, and racial socialization in rural, single-mother families with child self-worth and self-regulation. In H. P. McAdoo (Ed.), *Black children: Social, educational, and parental environments* (pp. 97–115). Thousand Oaks: Sage.

Mylonakou, I., & Kekes, I. (2005). Syneducation: Reinforcing communication and strengthening cooperation among students, parents, and schools. Harvard Family Research Project, Cambridge, MA. Retrieved 11/25/07 at: http://www.gse.harvard.edu/hfrp/projects/fine/resources/research/syneducation.html

Nicholls, J. G., & Miller, A. T. (1984). Reasoning about the ability of self and others: A developmental study. *Child Development, 55,* 1990–1999.

Ng, F. F., Kenney-Benson, G. A., & Pomerantz, E. M. (2004). Children's achievement moderates the effects of mothers' use of control and autonomy support. *Child Development, 75,* 764–780.

Phinney, J. (1993). A three-stage model of ethnic identity development in adolescence. In M.E. Bernal & G. P. Knight (Eds.), *Ethnic identity: Formation and transmission among hispanics and other minorities.* Albany NY: SUNY Press.

Phinney, J. (1996). When we talk about American ethnic groups, what do we mean? *American Psychologist, 51,* 918–927.

Piaget, J. (1983). Piaget's theory. In P. H. Mussen (Ed.), *Handbook of child psychology (4th Ed.), Vol. 1: History, theory and methods.* New York: Wiley.

Parent Institute for Quality Education (2008). Nine week parent involvement education program. Retrieved on 10/13/08 at: http://www.piqe.org/Assets/Home/nine_week_parent_involvement.htm

Selman, R. L. (1980). *The growth of interpersonal understanding: Developmental and clinical analysis.* New York: Academic Press.

Siegler, R. S. (1996). *Emerging minds: The process of change in children's thinking.* New York: Oxford University Press.

Simon, B. (2004). High school outreach and family involvement. *Social Psychology of Education, 7,* 1381–1390.

Simpson, A.R., & Roehlkepartain, E. C. (2003). Asset building in parenting practices and family life. In R. M. Lerner & P. L. Benson (Eds.), *Developmental assets and asset building communities* (pp. 157–193). New York: Kluwer Academic.

Smetana, J.G., Campione-Barr, N., & Metzger, A. (2006). Adolescent development in interpersonal and societal contexts. *Annual Review of Psychology, 57,* 255–284.

Smith, E.P., Gorman-Smith, D, Quinn, W.H. & Rabiner, D.L. (2004) Community-Based multiple family groups to prevent and reduce violent and aggressive behavior: The GREAT Families Program. *American Journal of Preventive Medicine, 26,* 39–47.

Sociometrics Corporation (2008). Statement of Capabilities. Retrieved 1/31/08 at: http://www.socio.com/pdf/soc.pdf

Spera, C. (2005). A review of the relationship among parenting practices, parenting styles, and adolescent school achievement, *Educational Psychology Review, 17,* 125–146.

Steinberg, L. (2001). We know some things: Adolescent–parent relationships in retrospect and prospect. *Journal of Research on Adolescence, 11,* 1–19.

Steinberg, L., & Morris, A. S. (2001). Adolescent Development. *Annual Review of Psychology, 52,* 83–110.

Sue, D., Mak, W. S., & Sue, D. W. (1998). Ethnic identity. In L. C. Lee, & N. W. S. Zane (Eds.), *Handbook of Asian American psychology* (pp. 289–323). Thousand Oaks: Sage.

Suizzo, M. A., Robinson, C. R., & Pahlke, E. (2008). African American mothers' socialization beliefs and goals with young children: Themes of history, struggle, education, and collective independence. *Journal of Family Issues, 29,* 287–316.

Suizzo, M. A., & Soon, K. (2006). Parental academic socialization: Effects of home-based parental involvement on locus of control across U.S. ethnic groups. *Educational Psychology, 26,* 827–846.

Tatum, B. D. (2004). Family life and school experiences: Factors in racial identity development of Black youth in White communities. *Journal of Social Issues, 60,* 117–135.

Taylor, L. C., Clayton, J. D., Rowley, S. J. (2004). Academic socialization: Understanding parental influences on children's school-related development, *Review of General Psychology, 8,* 163–178.

Tierney, W.G. (2002). Parents and families in precollege preparation: The lack of connection between research and practice. *Educational Policy, 16,* 558–606.

Turiel, E. (1998). The development of morality. In W. Damon & N. Eisenberg (Eds.) *Handbook of child psychology (5th Ed.) Vol 3: Social, emotional, and personality development* (pp. 863–932) New York: Wiley.

UC ANR Latino/a Teen Pregnancy Prevention Workgroup. (2004). *Best practices in teen pregnancy prevention: Practitioner handbook.* Oakland: UC Cooperative Extension.

Valdez, G. (1996). *Con respeto. Bridging the distances between culturally diverse families and schools: An ethnographic portrait.* New York: Teachers College.

Valencia, R. R. (1997). Conceptualizing the notion of deficit thinking. In R. R. Vaencia (Ed.) *The evolution of deficit thinking: Educational thought and practice.* London: Falmer.

Vidano, G. & Sahafi, M. (2004). Parent Institute for Quality Education Organization Special Report on PIQE's Performance Evaluation. San Diego State University, San Diego.

Wentzel, K. R. (1998). Parents' aspirations for children's educational attainments: Relations to parental beliefs and social address variables. *Merrill-Palmer Quarterly, 4,* 20–37.

Wigfield, A., & Eccles, J. S. (2002). The development of competence beliefs, expectancies for success, and achievement values from childhood through adolescence. In A. Wigfield & J. S. Eccles (Eds.), *The development of achievement motivation* (pp. 91–120). San Diego: Academic Press.

Wright, D. R. & Fitzpatrick, K. M. (2006). Violence and minority youth: The effects of asset factors on fighting among African American children and adolescents. *Adolescence, 41,* 251–262.

CHAPTER 3

THE ROLE OF FAMILY AND COMMUNITY IN EXTRACURRICULAR ACTIVITY PARTICIPATION

A Developmental Approach to Promoting Youth Participation in Positive Activities during the High School Years

Nicole Zarrett and Jacquelynne Eccles

INTRODUCTION

Although research suggests that youth will derive the greatest benefits from their out-of-school time by participating in organized extracurricular activities (see Mahoney, Larson, & Eccles, 2005), the selection process of getting youth involved and keeping youth involved in organized activities is complex. Specifically, activity choices involve reciprocal processes between the contextual constraints and opportunities for participation within the fam-

Promising Practices for Family and Community Involvement during High School, pages 27–51

ily, community, and adolescents' own motivations to participate (Bouffard, Wimer, & Caronongan et al., 2006; Elder & Conger, 2000; Mahoney et al., 2005). Moreover, the "fit" between the individual and the characteristics of the organized activity ("activity context"), including the presence and quality of the activity leaders, the types of participating peers, and special skill requirements, also act to promote or inhibit youth participation in the activity (Eccles & Gootman, 2002). The purpose of this chapter is to discuss the central factors that influence high school adolescents' extracurricular activity participation within a developmental theoretical framework that can help integrate and inform further research and practice. Through an examination of the factors that influence participation, we can identify ways to best promote youth engagement in positive activities during the nonschool hours.

Conceptualizing Activity Involvement

There are many classification schemes used for describing adolescent activity involvement. Researchers in leisure studies distinguish between constructive organized activities and passive leisure. Sports psychologists distinguish between competitive team-based and individual noncompetitive activities. Developmentalists distinguish between adult supervised versus unsupervised activities, structured versus unstructured time, in-school and out-of-school activities, and prosocial and antisocial activities. Educators distinguish among extracurricular, co-curricular, and academic activities. Even within developmental psychology, there are many classification schemes for activities based on: the time and place in which the activity occurs (in-school versus after-school programs); who and how many are participating (solo activities, activities with peers, or activities with one's family); the nature of supervision (whether it exists and who supervises it); the amount of structure (structured and unstructured); the intent of the activity (to teach skills or provide opportunities for play); and the content domain itself (music, reading, sports, work, watching TV, hanging out). Activities can be classified using many different systems. For example, organized team sports and instrumental music lessons tend to be structured, supervised, and skill-based activities; art activities and reading for pleasure tend to be less structured and unsupervised but still skill-based; hanging out with friends at a neighborhood park tends to be unstructured, unsupervised, and likely nonskill-based.

Among all of these various ways of classifying activities however, there is a strong distinction between the constructive ways adolescents spend their time (which we refer to as "constructive activities") and the unconstructive (ineffectual) activities in which youth engage. Constructive activities include all activities that provide youth challenge and opportunities for skill building. These activities are often voluntary and participation requires concerted effort and engagement by the youth, usually over an extended period of time (Eccles & Gootman, 2002; Larson, 2000; Roth & Brooks-Gunn, 2003). Therefore, youth get involved and stay invested in constructive activities because of their intrinsic interest and enjoyment in the activity. In fact, researchers have found that youth who spend their free time participating in these activities report experiencing high challenge, concentration, and motivation; a combination of experiences classified as the highest form of intrinsic motivation, and a combination of experiences rarely reported when engaged in other activities in their lives, for example, during school-based activities, watching television, or hanging out with friends (Larson, 2000).

Youth participate in constructive activities that are available within their schools and neighborhoods (sports, school government, YMCA), within their families (household chores, family picnics, and so forth), and even during their time spent alone, for example, practicing a musical instrument, doing homework, playing video games. In particular, organized constructive activities (which we refer to as *extracurricular* activities throughout the remainder of this chapter), such as participating in the school debate club or scouts, have become increasingly recognized for their major influence on adolescent development (Mahoney et al., 2005). Organized extracurricular activities engage youth in a distinct set of socializing experiences, including a distinguished set of behaviors, rules, scripts and goals. In addition, these activities are focused on developing a particular set of skills and take place in distinct settings, with regularly scheduled meetings and the supervision and guidance from adults, to aid youth in achieving the goals of the activity.

The structure inherent in organized extracurricular activities has enabled researchers to study in great length the nature and effects of participating in these activities and the settings in which they take place. Participation in these activities have been associated with positive adolescent and adult outcomes such as reduced rates of delinquency, higher academic and occupational achievement, and the development of identity and initiative (Larson, Walker, & Pearce, 2005; Lauver, Little, & Weiss, 2004; Mahoney, 2000; Barber, Eccles, & Stone, 2001).

While some adolescents will have considerable opportunities, means, and social supports available to facilitate their participation in a diversity of organized extracurricular activities, multiple and co-effecting constraints will restrict the activity options available to other youth (Lareau, 2003; National Research Council and Institute of Medicine, 2002). Research has shown that youth who do not participate in any organized extracurricular activities, and spend much of their nonschool hours engaged in unconstructive activities such as watching noneducational television or cruising in cars with friends are at risk for poor psychosocial and achievement-related functioning (Eccles, Barber, Stone, & Hunt, 2003; Feinstein, Bynner, & Duckworth, 2006; Mahoney, Stattin, & Lord, 2004).

This chapter focuses on examining the factors that support adolescents' initial and continued engagement in organized extracurricular activities during their nonschool hours. Participation can contribute to the development of important cognitive, social, and psychological assets, and prevent youth from the possible detrimental developmental effects of spending too much of their free time in unconstructive activities.

Theoretical Framework

Adolescents' extracurricular activity participation can be best understood through a Dynamic Systems perspective on human development (see Baltes, 1997; Bronfenbrenner, 2005; Eccles, Wigfield, & Schiefele, 1998; Lerner, 2006; Magnusson & Stattin, 2006; Overton, 2006 for examples of the conceptualization and application of this theoretical framework). According to the Dynamic Systems perspective development occurs as the result of a system of interactions within the individual and between the individual and their complex ecology over time. A direct implication of this proposition is that understanding adolescent development requires that the network of relations between characteristics of the individual and the ecologies in which he/she develops must be studied in an integrated and temporal manner (Magnusson & Stattin, 2006). Moreover, this idea of a multilevel developmental system emphasizes the potential for change both in the individual and the contexts in which individuals develop in the service of promoting positive development.

In particular, Bronfenbrenner (2005) developed the Bioecological Model as a framework for looking at child socialization as resulting from dynamic interactions between individuals and the various levels of their environment. The environments in which Bronfenbrenner referenced included everything from the distal influences of state and federal policy to the more proximal environments that adolescents are of one part, called "microsystems," such as the school and family. He emphasized the bidirectional relations of contextual systems whereby material and social resources at each level promote or inhibit adolescents' participation, engagement, and learning. Bronfenbrenner and Morris (2006) noted that the direct person–context interactions that occurred at the "microsystem" level were of particular importance. Although more distal ecologies, such as the parents' workplace, or a federal policy, influence the type and quality of interactions that occur within the microsystem, development is directly influenced by the moment-to-moment pattern of exchange between the individual and his/her surroundings.

Applying the Bioecological Model to youth motivation to engage in extracurricular activities leads us to stress the importance of examining the connected nature between youth and the social and material influences that characterize their various daily contexts. Furthermore, within the Bioecological Model each part of the system (such as the individual, their family, peer group, neighborhood) is considered to be only one important part of a complex multilevel system. Therefore, if we are to understand what gets youth engaged in positive extracurricular activities, we must consider simultaneously *all* of the parts of the developmental system and how they interact with one another to promote youth activity participation.

This bidirectional (interactional) process that occurs between different parts of the system is observed in the Eccles' Expectancy-Value model (Eccles, 1983), and its extension (Eccles, 1993) that can be seen in Figure 3.1. The Eccles' Expectancy-Value model is founded on the premise that activity-related choices are directly linked to whether the individual attaches importance to the activity (value), and whether they feel they are good at, and expect future success in the activity (expectancy). Eccles and her colleagues have identified multiple factors that contribute to individuals' development of these expectancies and values that cut across multiple ecological levels. As seen in Figure 3.1, an individual's activity choices and their activity-specific beliefs, values, and behaviors (Box H) are both influential on, and influenced by parent behaviors (Box E, F, and G) and beliefs (Box C, and D), which are all influenced by the resources and supports in the family (Box A) and child (assets, Box B), as well as the neighborhood and schools (not indicated), and the broader cultural milieu. All levels play a key role in determining how individuals select into activities (Eccles, 1993). In this chapter we review what we know about each of these parts of the system (important youth microsystems), and the ways they interact to influence adolescents' participation in extracurricular activities during the high school years.

PREDICTORS OF PARTICIPATION

Adolescents' participation in organized extracurricular activities is the result of a complex set of processes. Participation in organized activities first depends on whether youth have access to activities within their communities (schools and neighborhoods). However, even where a variety of organized activities are available to youth, there remains significant variability in whether adolescents participate in these activities. Researchers are beginning to unravel the individual and contextual predictors of participation.

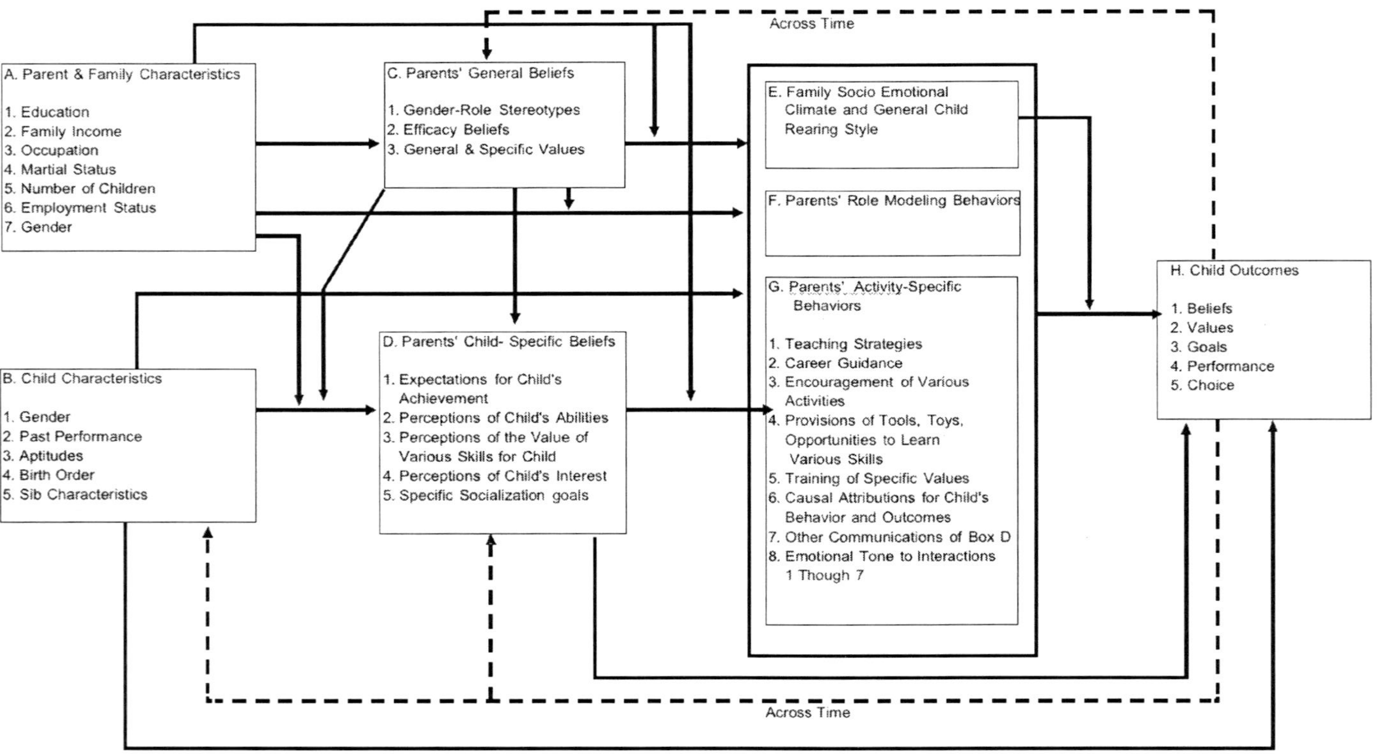

Figure 3.1 Model of parents' influence on children's achievement related to self-perception, values, amd behaviors.

Youth Indicators

According to the Bioecological perspective, a child is seen as an active and purposeful agent in the developmental process; characteristics of the whole child both affect and are affected by the interactions that occur within and across their various ecologies in a reciprocal fashion across development. Therefore, in order to examine factors that influence adolescents' extracurricular time-use choices, we must first understand the person-level factors that influence choice and behavior.

Beyond general indicators of youth functioning, such as their academic achievement (Marsh & Kleitman, 2002), social competence (e.g., Mahoney, Cairns, & Farmer, 2003; Persson, Kerr, & Stattin, 2007), and overall adjustment (Busseri, Rose-Krasnor, Willoughby, & Chalmers, 2006), adolescents' self-concept of ability and interest (value) in an activity have been identified both theoretically and empirically as the strongest predictors of youth activity participation (Ryan & Deci, 2000; Wigfield & Eccles, 2002). Multiple psychological theories (such as attribution theory, self-efficacy theory) suggest that youth are more motivated to select increasingly challenging tasks when they feel that they have the ability to accomplish such tasks (Ryan & Deci, 2000; Bandura, 1997). In terms of activity participation, this means that if an adolescent feels highly competent in playing a soccer game in gym class then s/he will likely be motivated to continue playing soccer, and seek other more competitive venues as his or her skills developed. Research has provided ample empirical evidence that ability beliefs are related to achievement and long-term engagement in a variety of domains, even after controlling for previous achievement or ability (Eccles, Wigfield, Harold, & Blumenfeld, 1993).

Adolescents also enroll and persist in an activity because of their expressed value of, or interest in, the activity (Luthar, Shoum, & Brown, 2006; Scanlan, Babkes, & Scanlan, 2005). In fact, several studies have provided support for the strong relation between adolescents' self-concept of ability and values (see Jacobs, Lanza, Osgood, Eccles, & Wigfield, 2002; Harter, 1998; Wigfield & Eccles, 2002). This research has found that if an individual also values the activity for which they feel competent, s/he will experience high levels of motivation to participate. For example, using a longitudinal design, Barber, Jacobson, Eccles, and Horn (1997) found that ratings of enjoyment, perceived importance, and self-concept of ability in sports during the tenth grade predicted persistence in sports two years later. Moreover, Jacobs and colleagues (2002) found that the relations between adolescents' self-concept of ability, interest, and their participation in the activity are reciprocal across time.

Early participation (during middle childhood and adolescence), where youth build their activity-specific skill set and increased internal motivation, predicts sustained participation (Busseri et al., 2006; Jordan & Nettles, 2000; Mahoney et al., 2003) even when activities become competitive in high school (Quiroz, 2000; Simpkins, Ripke, Huston, & Eccles, 2005). However, internal motivations (values and ability beliefs) often develop as a result of participation due to external motivating factors (Pearce & Larson, 2006). The influence of other people, including encouraging parents, participating friends, teachers, and coaches are common external reasons that adolescents provide for why they first enrolled in the activity (Loder & Hirsch, 2003). Other external motivators include school requirements (Pearce & Larson, 2006), and resume building, as youth enter the later adolescent years (Quiroz, 2000). In contrast, adolescents' negative responses to an activity, such as stress, have been shown to lead to decreased motivation and drop out (Scanlan et al., 2005).

In line with the Dynamic Systems framework more research is needed to address how a combination of internal and external motivational factors is at work in adolescents' initial and continued engagement in extracurricular activities (Zarrett, 2007). Some recent research has shown that the various different types of motivation (such as interest, friends) are predictive of adolescents' experiences during the activity (Hansen & Larson, 2007); such that, adolescents who attended because of interest and future goals report having more developmental experiences during the activity.

Family Socialization

The socialization process that occurs within families has been studied for decades and recognized for the prominent role it plays in child and adolescent development (Collins, Maccoby, Steinberg et al., 2000). Parents provide needed resources and encouragement to promote and sustain youth participation in activities. Along with parent education, occupation, and income (SES) (Bartko & Eccles, 2003), and the selection of neighborhoods and schools often reflective of parents' SES (Parke, Killian, Dennis et al., 2003), previous research indicates that parents' activity beliefs and behaviors also play an important role in children's initial engagement and continued pursuit of activities. Much research on parent socialization has focused on parents' beliefs and behaviors as critical components in setting a climate for children's motivation development (expectancies and values) (Eccles, 1993; Eccles et al., 1998). This research has identified three parenting mechanisms by which parents influence their children's activity participation: role modeling, direct provision of activity-related experiences (including support and encouragement), and their own beliefs about the activity (most prominently, the degree to which they believe their child is competent in the activity and how much they view the activity as important). We discuss these three in terms of two more general concepts: parents as interpreters of their children's experience and parents as providers of experience.

Parents as Interpreters of Experience

Parents help interpret their children's experiences by relaying messages to their children about the value of the activity and their likelihood of attaining future success engaging in the activity. Where academics, especially through the middle school years, does not allow youth much choice (required to complete particular course work), participation in an extracurricular activity is much more voluntary and therefore, more likely under the influence of such motivational factors. Using longitudinal data, Eccles and her colleagues found much empirical support for the hypothesized causal relations between parents' beliefs and children's self and task beliefs (e.g., Eccles et al., 1998; Goodnow & Collins, 1990; Jacobs, Vernon, & Eccles, 2005). For example, parents' ability and value beliefs predict their children's value and perceptions of ability in sports as well as the amount of time they spend playing sports, net of the effect of the children's actual motor skill abilities (Simpkins, Fredricks, Davis-Kean, & Eccles, 2006). Furthermore, parents' expectations of their children's athletic ability in the elementary school years was shown to predict changes in their children's sports self-concepts from first grade through high school (Fredricks & Eccles, 2005). Youth evidenced less dramatic declines in their self-concept of sport ability if they had parents who had high expectations for their children's success in sports.

Parents as Providers of Experience

Parents also influence their adolescents' motivational beliefs and behaviors by providing various experiences and resources that provide exposure and encouragement to pursue activities across time. Such support can include parents participating along with their adolescent in the activity (co-activity), which gives parents the opportunity to actively coach and teach their children skills, and to provide performance feedback including direct positive and negative reinforcements for participating. Moreover, parents' involvement in their adolescents' activities further relays messages to their children about the relative importance of the activity, where high rates of involvement communicate high importance. In contrast, low parental involvement (less emotional, financial, or functional investment in their child's activities) is likely to undermine youth interest and engagement in such activities (Fredricks & Eccles, 2005; Horn, 1987).

Parents can also act as role models with active engagement in their own set of activities. In fact, research suggests both concurrent relations between parent and youth activity levels (Babkes & Weiss, 1999) and longitudinal influences of parents' own activity involvement on their child's subsequent participation in the activity through adolescence (Huebner & Mancini, 2003; Simpkins, Davis-Kean, & Eccles, 2005). Lastly, parents can encourage their children's participation by watching their adolescent participate in the activity (be a "cheerleader"), and by taking their children to activity-specific events (for example, a baseball game, the opera, a rock concert).

Few studies have considered the different ways parents combine these socialization techniques, and subsequent variations in youth participation. Researchers who have examined these relations have concluded that the greater the number of supports a parent provides the greater the likelihood of youth participation (Fredricks & Eccles, 2002; Zarrett, 2007). However, parents may not be able to provide a number of supports, given they must also face their own set of barriers and constraints. Therefore, recent research has begun to examine what specific types of supports, in combination with one another, are essential to promote youth engagement in extracurricular activities (Zarrett, 2007; Zarrett, Peck, & Eccles, 2007).

Quality of Parental Involvement

Research has also shown that the quality of parents' involvement is important. For example, concerns have been raised about parents' excessive involvement in their child and his/her activities, especially when parents emphasize winning, place too much pressure on their children to succeed, or express high levels of frustration with their children when they fail to meet parents' standards of success (Williams & Lester, 2000). Parents' frustration with their adolescents' performance in an activity was found to decrease the likelihood that their children would continue to engage in the activity (Brustad, 1996). High levels of parental pressure predicted adolescents' higher levels of stress and anxiety prior to and during participation, lower-motivation to engage in the activity, and burnout. In contrast, lower levels of parental pressure predicted greater enjoyment in the activity (Babkes & Weiss, 1999; Brustad 1996).

Parents' mental health and parenting style can also influence adolescents' activity participation. For example, an authoritative parenting style, and parent warmth were found to predict higher participation in constructive activities and lower participation in unconstructive activities (Bohnert, Martin, & Garber, 2007; Huebner & Mancini, 2003; Persson et al., 2007). Researchers believe that these more general parenting behaviors impact youth participation indirectly, by promoting adolescents' socioemotional adjustment and academic achievement, although these mediation models have not been tested.

Lastly, where research has evidenced a much stronger causal relation of parents' influence on child beliefs and behaviors than the reverse, studies on parent–child relations indicate that children, through their expressed interest, ability, and behaviors, have at least some influence on parents' socialization behaviors and beliefs. Therefore, it is also likely that youth prompt parents to provide the socioemotional and material resources needed to pursue the activity, through their expressed interests and demonstration of ability (e.g., Belsky & Park, 2000; Darling & Steinberg, 1993; Jacobs et al., 2005). Additional research is needed that examines the reciprocal nature of the socialization process that occurs between youth and their parents, for getting youth involved in extracurricular activities.

Sibling Influence

Within the family, siblings can also influence each other's development beyond that accounted for by the contributions of shared genetics and parenting (Slomkowski, Rende, Novak et al., 2005). Typically, younger siblings are influenced by their older siblings who function as both role models and as providers of opportunities and experiences (Whiteman, McHale, & Crouter, 2007). For example, researchers have shown that through social and observational learning mechanisms (Bandura, 1977), namely modeling and imitation, younger siblings often engage in similar risk behaviors as their older sibling (Ary, Tildesley, Hops, & Andrews, 1993; Windle, 2000). Younger siblings observe what behaviors and activities receive praise or reinforcement by peers and parents, and engage in those that appear to garner the greatest benefit (McHale, Updegraf, Jackson-Newsom et al., 2000). In addition, older siblings function as "gatekeepers" providing the settings, resources, and opportunities for younger siblings to engage in these behaviors, as well as a network of influential peers who act as additional models and partners in navigating these new behaviors (see Whiteman et al., 2007 for review). However, research on the extent to which these processes operate and influence youth extracurricular activity participation has been rarely measured.

In a recent study, Whiteman and colleagues (2007) assessed the link between adolescents' perceptions of sibling influence and sibling similarities in athletic interests and artistic interests. Their findings show that younger siblings share similar activity interests as their older siblings when they viewed their older sibling as highly influential, and when the older sibling was highly interested in the activity. This study is the first to examine some of the processes involved in sibling influences on youth activity participation. Much research is still needed to identify the longitudinal nature of these relations. Moreover, there is little to no research on how younger siblings influence their older sibling's behaviors or activity preferences. There has been much more research on the nature of peer influence on youth activity choices more generally.

Peers and Family Socialization

The relation between activity participation and peers, often referred to as a "leisure culture", and its link to developmental outcomes has been well documented (Eccles et al., 2003; Kinney, 1993; Mahoney et al., 2003). Much empirical research has shown that adolescents' friend groups ("crowd"), and the social identities they attach to this affiliation, are critical predictors of the types of activities in which adolescents participate (Eccles & Barber, 1999; Huebner & Mancini, 2003; Luthar et al., 2006). Common documented examples of this association include participation in sports and affiliation with the "jock" crowd, and participation in school spirit clubs and affiliation with the "populars" crowd. Moreover, youth report "spending time with friends" as a central motivating factor for why they first chose to participate in an activity, their enjoyment in the activity, and whether they persist or dropout of an activity (Borden, Perkins, Villarruel, & Stone, 2005; Persson et al., 2007).

Therefore, family influence on their adolescents' peer relationships has important implications for the types of activities in which youth participate during their nonschool hours and must be considered as an additional source of influence in our research paradigms. Where siblings provide one another a network of influential peers (Whiteman et al., 2007), parent monitoring of their adolescents' peer relationships has been identified as the primary way parents influence their adolescents' friendships (Parke & O'Neil, 1999). Through enabling and restricting access to particular peers, parents' ensure that their adolescent will not get involved with deviant peers during the adolescent years (Brown, Mounts, Lamborn & Steinberg, 1993; Mounts, 2002). Research has shown that adolescents who have more friends that are a positive influence (value school, obey their parents) are more likely to participate in a wider variety of extracurricular activities (Simpkins & Becnel, 2007). Parental monitoring is thus a particularly effective indirect means for encouraging their adolescents' activity participation.

Community

The community in which youth reside is another "microsystem" we must consider for its direct impact on adolescents' extracurricular activity participation. Safe, nurturing, and caring environments enable youth to explore a variety of options and roles, facilitate the development of positive mentor relationships, and contribute to the development of adolescents' personal assets (e.g., self-esteem, social skills). In contrast, social isolation, concentrated poverty, and public neglect, the fabric of many U.S. neighborhoods and their school systems, contain many risks that can challenge adolescents' positive development (Dunbar, 2002; Roffman, Suaurez-Orozco, & Rhodes, 2003). The development of multilevel techniques in the past decade has made it possible to statistically estimate relations between neighborhood-level characteristics and individual outcomes. This research has demonstrated that access to youth activity contexts is significantly associated with increases in youth participation. Neighborhood resources, such as parks, community centers, playing fields, and positive adult mentors that implement and oversee the activity, are a necessity for such participation. Within economically disadvantaged urban neighborhoods and poor, isolated rural areas, where youth have the greatest needs for developmental supports, these types of provisions are often sparse (e.g., Duncan & Brooks-Gunn, 2000; Rural School & Community Trust, 2005; Save the Children, 2002). For example, nationally representative studies (e.g., National Educational Longitudinal Study), have shown that economically disadvantaged communities, with less public support and funding, have fewer youth organizations, sport leagues, summer camps, and out-of-school programs than more affluent communities (Hirsch, Roffman, Deutsch et al., 2000; Quinn, 1999). Youth from such low-income neighborhoods attend schools that also have limited economic resources and are less equipped to provide the variety and quality of extracurricular programming that is typically available to youth attending schools in wealthier neighborhoods (Pedersen & Seidman, 2005).

Moreover, adolescents' communities must be considered as only one part of an integrated system that includes youth and their other microsystems (such as family, peers). For instance, many youth have limited access to the activities that are available in their communities because of family constraints and concerns. Extracurricular activities can be costly, involving enrollment fees, uniforms, instruments, and other equipment, and require transportation which can be difficult for parents who are under financial strain and rigorous, erratic work schedules (Casey, Ripke, & Huston, 2005). Where there are youth programs and other affordable extracurricular activities provided in low-income communities, issues of safety and access often remain primary sources of deterrence to youth participation. For example, in some neighborhoods children will need to walk toward and through highly disordered, high crime areas in order to attend activities at their local community center, school, or park. In such cases, many parents limit their child's attendance in youth programs to avoid exposure to these risks (Fauth, Roth, & Brooks-Gunn, 2007; Jarrett, 1997; Shann, 2001). Using neighborhood observation data from the Project on Human Development in Chicago Neighborhoods (Earls & Buka, 1997), Molnar, Gortmaker, Bull, and Buka, (2004) have provided much evidence in support of this issue, showing that much of the variation in levels of youth physical activity across neighborhoods was accounted for by neighborhood social disorder and lack of safety.

Even across economically diverse neighborhoods and schools, the size of the school also makes a difference in terms of access. Although larger schools typically offer a greater number of activities, participation rates are lower at large schools because the ratio of open slots to the student population is more favorable in a small school than a large school (Jordan & Nettles, 2000; Quiroz, 2000). The activities available and accessible to young people also depend more generally on country locale. Although urban youth have to contend with issues of safety, youth in rural environments have more limited opportunities for activities than their counterparts. Furthermore, activities available to rural youth are often not situated locally in their town or school, resulting in a greater reliance on transport to access them. The limited public transport and larger distances to access activities in rural settings has the greatest impact on the extracurricular activity participation rates of poor rural youth (Storey & Brannen, 2000).

Differences in community supports, and the level in which these supports meet the needs of youth and their families, also impact individuals' orientation towards, and selection into, certain activities. In particular, low-income families are more likely to take advantage of activity opportunities offered by their religious institutions and local community centers than those offered by other institutions (such as the school) because they tend to be more affordable, more readily available, and easier to access in their communities (Simpkins et al., 2005b)

The Activity Context

In addition to availability and access, the opportunities and overall quality of the activity settings offered to youth within their communities is also an essential element for promoting youth participation in extracurricular activities. In order to determine the quality of an activity setting we must consider the relation between the activity context and the individual, or what has been termed the "person–environment fit" (Eccles et al., 1993; Erikson, 1968; Hunt, 1975; Magnusson & Stattin, 1998). From this perspective, individuals have needs that require appropriate responses from their social contexts in order to support healthy development. In the case of extracurricular activities, a context where participation is highly voluntary, youth will select into, or out of activities depending on whether these needs are met.

Among the most basic of these needs is physical safety, and individuals' socioemotional needs for achievement (competence), relatedness, and autonomy (Ryan & Deci, 2000). Researchers have proposed that successful extracurricular activities (both in terms of adolescent enrollment/retention rates, and the promotion of positive development) are those which provide intellectually challenging experiences, including the opportunity to acquire and practice specific social, physical, and intellectual skills that are useful in a wide variety of settings. Youth also seek out contexts that feel physically safe, and where it is safe to share their ideas (e.g., Borden et al., 2005; Lauver & Little, 2005). These activity settings provide a place where youth feel accepted and have the freedom to explore social and personal identities (free of racism and cultural intolerance) (Barber, Stone, Hunt, & Eccles, 2005) and their passions (Csikszentmihalyi & Kleiber, 1991). Successful activities provide youth a sense of belonging to a socially recognized and valued group where they can establish supportive social networks of prosocial peers and adults that can help in both current and future goals (Eccles & Gootman, 2002), and enable youth to contribute to the well-being of their community and develop a sense of agency as a member of the community (Lerner, 2004; Youniss, McLellan, Su, & Yates, 1999).

Moreover, relationships with staff and learning experiences influence adolescents' continued interest (Pearce & Larson, 2006). In particular, research has found that staff who exhibit interaction styles similar to the authoritative parenting style is associated with higher adolescent interest in the activity (Cumming, Smith, & Smoll, 2006; Pearce & Larson, 2006); and a decrease in their negative reactions to the environment (such as stress; Scanlan et al., 2005).

Collectively, these basic needs and identities constitute important influences on what gets youth into, and keeps them engaged in extracurricular activities. Moreover, using person–environment fit as a point of departure, we must also elaborate this model by considering developmental changes. Incorporating information about developmental change into the person–environment fit model yields a "stage–environment fit" model that addresses how personal and social changes across *developmental time* impact the person–environment fit equation (Eccles & Midgley, 1989). Activity contexts that are appropriate for adolescents are not necessarily appropriate for children. Programs developed to cater to the needs of children and adolescents must map on to their growing maturity and expertise. For example, as youth move through the middle to late adolescent years communities must provide programs that map onto the new courses they are taking in school, their increasing cognitive capacities and identity concerns, and their movement towards adulthood, including a focus on future plans and the support to set and attain high educational and occupational goals (Eccles & Gootman, 2002; Zarrett & Eccles, 2006). Activities that are appropriate in terms of skill level and adolescent needs (such as opportunities for leadership) promote participation (Lauver & Little, 2005; Pearce & Larson, 2006) by optimizing adolescent learning and motivation (Ryan & Deci, 2000; Rogoff, 2003).

Ultimately, the most common attributes adolescents seek in an activity are that it is fun and interesting (Loder & Hirsch, 2003; Sharp, Pocklington, & Weindling, 2002). Adolescents bring their own set of values, interests, identity needs, and previous socialization experiences to their activity choices. Therefore, different activities, each with their own set of tasks, skills, goals, and general structure, will appeal to different youth. This is critical to enrollment. Any model of out-of-school time use that hopes to provide youth with the kinds of developmentally appropriate supports required to promote healthy development will need to attend explicitly to these human capacities, potentials, and needs and how they change over time during the course of development. Much research is still needed to understand the processes that occur within the activity setting, and how these processes help facilitate youth engagement and development (Vandell, Shumow, & Posner, 2005).

CONCLUSIONS: WHAT IS NEEDED TO GET YOUTH INVOLVED

Research has demonstrated that organized activities are settings in which adolescents are active agents in their own development. The activities in which adolescents choose to participate reflect core aspects of their self-beliefs, identification and a connection with the values and goals represented by the activity and shared by those who participate (e.g., school support/spirit), affiliation (or desire to be affiliated) with a particular peer group and social identity; and aspirations towards future selves (e.g., Dishion, Poulin, & Burraston, 2001; Eccles et al., 2003). When an activity setting meets adolescents' needs and interests, they remain engaged in the activity. Simultaneously, the activity context confirms adolescents' views of themselves and their worlds, and facilitates further development of their self-beliefs and values, social and personal identities, and social network (Jacobs et al., 2005). The longer an adolescent engages in the activity, the more they identify and become integrated within the peer culture, and the expected roles, values, and goals associated with the activity context.

Socialization into activities also follows similar bidirectional processes. For example, adolescents are both influenced and influence parents' beliefs about their adolescent's activity-specific abilities and perceptions of the value of the activity context in their adolescent's life. Parents also encourage their adolescent's participation in the activity through other socializing behaviors, such as providing materials for participation, transportation to and from the activity, and parents' own participation in the activity (Eccles, 1993). Lastly, parents must know that activity opportunities exist in their communities, and reassured that they are safe, nurturing settings for their adolescent. Therefore, outreach from the community, and the involvement of parents, are both needed to help youth make activity choices that will benefit them.

In addition to considering the relations across levels of the system, it is just as important to consider the complex interactions of characteristics within each level of the system. For example, at the level of the youth, perceiving an activity as important will likely not promote involvement in the activity unless this perceived value is paired with adolescents' belief that they are good at the activity, and that these beliefs are equal or more positive for the particular activity than other activities in which they can choose. Adolescents' general psychological well-being and motivational-orientation to engage in positive activities are also as important for youth participation. Likewise, at the family and community levels, one supportive factor is not likely to be enough to promote youth activity participation. Instead, various combinations of supports are needed to provide a supportive environment for youth to participate in an activity.

Youth who are provided fewer opportunities for participation in activities have less developmental opportunities than youth who have access to these programs (Quinn, 1999; Mahoney, 2000). The lower participation rates of adolescents of minority status and those from lower socioeconomic backgrounds and single-parent families remain of particular concern (Pedersen & Seidman, 2005; Shann, 2001) at a time when schools and communities are cutting extracurricular activities to compensate for nationwide budget shortfalls (Seidman & Pedersen, 2003). Cutting programs, or instilling and increasing activity fees, may be costly in the long term if such fees keep youth from participating in activities that can promote their healthy development. This is especially true for those youth who reside in high-risk neighborhoods, with less access to resources, and fewer contexts which can provide such support.

In contrast, investments in community building that identify, integrate, and maintain assets for healthy development will result in both the positive development of youth and thriving communities. Welfare reforms that increase parental employment, income, and/or publicly supported programs that are available close to adolescents' homes and schools, have been shown to facilitate children's participation in activities, providing these youth developmentally enriching experiences in supervised settings (Bos, Huston, Granger, Duncan et al., 1999).

To better realize the potentials of activity programs, we need more in-depth qualitative and longitudinal research that evaluates the mediating processes both within and between categories of activities (Larson, Hansen, & Moneta, 2006), as well as more dynamic models that account for the synergistic relations between youth, their environments, and activities. Although extensive work has taken into account particular components of the Dynamic Systems models discussed, very few studies have looked at youth and their various environments (microsystems) simultaneously. Zarrett, Peck, and Eccles (2007) have begun to investigate the several interacting components that characterize youth and each of their contexts (within-level influences) and the interaction between these various levels of the developmental system in the service of promoting youth extracurricular activity participation (Zarrett, 2007; Zarrett et al., 2007). This work suggests two key messages for future research and practice. The first implication of this research is that youth activity participation results from a dynamic, integrated, person-in-context system that involves the integrated support of adolescents' multiple microsystems. Therefore, we must address the degree of support available to youth at each level of the system if we are to promote youth participation in activities. The second major implication of this work is that activity participation provides youth an additional set of supports that promote youth development, beyond that accounted for by the personal assets and contextual supports responsible for getting youth engaged in activities (Zarrett, Peck, von Eye, & Eccles, under review). In basic terms, such findings indicate that extracurricular activities are an important ingredient in promoting adolescents' positive development, and that community and family supports to get youth involved in these activities are necessary if we are to nurture youth development.

REFERENCES

Ary, D. V., Tildesley, E., Hops, H., & Andrews, J. (1993). The influence of parent, sibling, and peer modeling and attitudes on adolescent use of alcohol. *International Journal of Addiction, 28,* 853–880.

Babkes, M. L., & Weiss, M. R. (1999). Parent influence on cognitive and affective responses in children's competitive soccer participation. *Pediatric Exercise Science, 11,* 44–62.

Baltes, P. B. (1997). On the incomplete architecture of human ontogeny: Selection, optimization, and compensation as foundations of developmental theory. *American Psychologist, 52,* 366–380.

Bandura, A. (1977). *Social learning theory.* Englewood Cliffs, NJ: Prentice Hall.

Bandura, A. (1997). *Self-efficacy: The exercise of control.* New York: W. H. Freeman & Co.

Barber, B. L., Eccles, J. S., & Stone, M. R. (2001). Whatever happened to the Jock, the Brain, and the Princess? Young adult pathways linked to adolescent activity involvement and social identity. *Journal of Adolescent Research, 16,* 429–455.

Barber, B. L., Jacobson, K. C., Eccles, J. S., & Horn, M. C. (1997). *"I don't want to play any more": When do talented adolescents drop out of competitive athletics?* Paper presented at the biennial meeting of the Society for Research on Child Development, Washington, DC.

Barber, B. L., Stone, M. R., Hunt, J. E., & Eccles, J. S. (2005). Benefits of activity participation: The roles of identity affirmation and peer group norm sharing. In J.L. Mahoney, R.W. Larson, & J.S. Eccles (Eds.) *Organized activities as contexts of development* (pp. 185–210). Mahwah, NJ: Lawrence Erlbaum Associates.

Bartko, T. W. & Eccles, J. S. (2003). Adolescent participation in structured and unstructured activities: A person-oriented analysis. *Journal of Youth and Adolescence, 32*(4), 233–241.

Belsky, J., & Park, S. (2000). Exploring reciprocal parent and child effects in the case of child inhibition in US and Korean samples. *International Journal of Behavioral Development, 24,* 3, 338–347.

Bohnert, A. M., Martin, N. C., Garber, J. (2007). Predicting adolescents' organized activity involvement: The role of maternal depression history, family relationship quality, and adolescent cognitions. *Journal of Research on Adolescence, 17*(1), 221–244.

Borden, L. M., Perkins, D. F., Villarruel, F. A., & Stone, M. R. (2005). To participate or not to participate: That is the question. In G. G. Noam (Ed.). H. B. Weiss, P. M. D. Little, and S. M. Bouffard (Issue Eds.). *New Directions for Youth Development. No. 105: Participation in youth programs: Enrollment, attendance, and engagement,* 33–50.

Bos, J. M., Huston, A. C., Granger, R. C., Duncan, G. J., Brock, T. W., & McLoyd, V. C. (1999). *New hope for people with low income: Two-year results of a program to reduce poverty and reform welfare.* New York: Manpower Demonstration Research Corporation.

Bouffard, S., Wimer, C., Caronongan, P., Little, P., Dearing, E., & Simpkins, S. D. (2006). Demographic differences in patterns of youth out-of-school time activity participation. *Journal of Youth Development.* Available at http://www.nae4ha.org/directory/jyd/intro.html

Bronfenbrenner, U. (2005). *Making human beings human: Bioecological perspectives on human development.* Thousand Oaks, CA: Sage.

Bronfenbrenner, U., & Morris, P. (2006). The bioecological model of human development. In W. Daman & R. M. Lerner (Editors-in-Chief) and R. M. Lerner (Volume Ed.), *Handbook of child psychology: Vol 1. Theoretical models of human development* (pp. 793–828). Hoboken, NJ: John Wiley & Sons.

Brown, B. B., Mounts, N. S., Lamborn, S. D., & Steinberg, L. D.(1993). Parenting practices and peer group affiliation in adolescence. *Child Development, 64,* 467–482.

Brustad, R. J. (1996). Parental and peer influences on children's psychological development through sport. In F. L. Smoll & R. E. Smith (Eds.), *Children and youth sport: A biopsychosocial perspective* (pp. 112–124). Dubuque, IA: Brown & Benchmark.

Busseri, M. A., Rose-Krasnor, L., Willoughby, T., & Chalmers, H. (2006). A longitudinal examination of breadth and intensity of youth activity involvement and successful development. *Developmental Psychology, 42,* 1313–1326.

Casey, D. M., Ripke, M. N., & Huston, A. C. (2005). Activity participation and the well being of children and adolescents in the context of welfare reform. In J. L. Mahoney, R. W. Larson, & J. S. Eccles (Eds.), *Organized activities as contexts of development* (pp. 65–84). Mahwah, NJ: Erlbaum.

Collins, W. A., Maccoby, E., Steinberg, L., et al., (2000). Contemporary research on parenting: The case for nature and nurture. *American Psychologist, 55,* 218–232.

Csikszentmihalyi, M., & Kleiber, D. A. (1991). Leisure and self-actualization. In B. L. Driver, P. J. Brown, & G. L. Peterson (Eds.) *Benefits of leisure* (pp. 91–102). State College, PA: Venture.

Cumming, S. P., Smith, R. E., & Smoll, F. L. (2006). Athlete-perceived coaching behaviors: Relating two measurement traditions. *Journal of Sport and Exercise Psychology, 28*, 205 – 213.

Darling, N., & Steinberg, L. (1993). Parenting style as a context: An integrative model. *Psychological Bulletin, 113*(3), 487–496.

Dishion, T.J., Poulin, F., & Burraston, B. (2001). Peer group dynamics associated with iatrogenic effects in group interventions with high-risk young adolescents. In D.W. Nangle, & C.A. Erdley (Eds.) *The role of friendship in psychological adjustment.* (pp. 79–92). San Francisco, CA: Jossey-Bass/Pfeiffer.

Dunbar, C. (2002). *Alternative schooling for African American youth: Does anyone know we're here?* New York: Peter Lang.

Duncan, G.J., & Brooks-Gunn J. (2000). Family poverty, welfare reform, and child development. *Child Development, 71*(1), 188–196.

Earls, F. & Buka, S.L. (1997). *Project on Human Development in Chicago Neighborhoods: Technical Report.* Rockville, MD: National Institute of Justice.

Eccles, J. S. (1993). School and family effects on the ontogeny of children's interests, self-perceptions, and activity choice. In J. Jacobs (Ed.), *Nebraska symposium on motivation,1992: Developmental perspectives on motivation* (pp. 145–208). Lincoln: University of Nebraska Press.

Eccles, J. S. (1983). Expectancies, values, and academic behaviors. In J. Spence (Ed.), *Achievement and achievement motivation* (pp. 75–146). San Francisco: Freeman.

Eccles, J. S., & Barber, B. (1999). Student council, volunteering, basketball, or marching band: What kind of extracurricular participation matters? *Journal of Adolescent Research, 14*, 10 – 43.

Eccles, J. S., Barber, B. L., Stone, M., & Hunt, J. (2003). Extracurricular activities and adolescent development. *Journal of Social Issues, 59*(4), 865–889.

Eccles, J. S. & Gootman, J. A. (Eds.) (2002). Community programs to promote youth development. Washington, DC: National Academy Press.

Eccles, J. S. & Midgley, C. (1989). Stage/environment fit: Developmentally appropriate classrooms for early adolescents. In R. Ames & C. Ames (Eds.) *Research on motivation in education* (Vol 3, pp. 139–181). New York: Academic Press.

Eccles, J. S., Wigfield, A., & Schiefele, U. (1998). Motivation to succeed. In W. Damon (Series Ed.), & N. Eisenberg (Vol. Ed.), Handbook of child psychology: Vol. 3, Social, emotional and personality development (5th ed.), New York: Wiley, 1017–1094.

Eccles, J. S., Wigfield, A., Harold, R. D., & Blumenfeld, P. (1993). Age and gender differences in children's achievement self-perceptions during the elementary school years. *Child Development, 64*, 830–847.

Elder, G.H. & Conger, R. (2000). *Children of the land.* Chicago: University of Chicago Press.

Erikson, E. H. (1968). *Identity: Youth and Crisis.* New York: Norton.

Fauth, R. C., Roth, J. L., & Brooks-Gunn, J. (2007). Does the neighborhood context alter the link between youth's after-school time activities and developmental outcomes? A multilevel analysis. *Developmental Psychology, 43(3),* 760–777.

Feinstein, L., Bynner, J., & Duckworth, K. (2006) Young people's leisure contexts and their relation to adult outcomes. *Journal of Youth Studies,* 9(3), 305–327.

Fredricks, J. A. & Eccles, J. S. (2005). Family socialization, gender, and sport motivation and involvement. *Journal of Sport & Exercise Psychology, 27,* 3–31.

Fredricks, J. A. & Eccles, J. S. (2002). Children's competence and value beliefs from childhood through adolescence: Growth trajectories in two male-sex-typed domains. *Developmental Psychology, 38*(4), 519–533.

Friedman, S., & Lichter, D. T. (1998). Spatial inequality and poverty among American children. Population research and policy review, 17(2), 91–109.

Garton, A. F., & Pratt, C. (1987). Participation and interest in leisure activities by adolescent school children. *Journal of Adolescence, 10,* 341–351.

Goodnow, J. J., & Collings, W. A. (1990). Development according to parents: The nature, sources, and consequences of parents' ideas. Hillsdale, NJ: Lawrence Erlbaum.

Hansen, D. M. & Larson, R. W. (2007). Amplifiers of developmental and negative experiences in organized activities: Dosage, motivation, lead roles, and adult-youth ratios. *Journal of Applied Developmental Psychology, 28(4),* 360–374.

Harter, S. (1998). The development of self-representations. In N. Eisenberg (Ed.), W. Damon (Series Ed.), *Handbook of child psychology: Vol 3. Social emotional, and personality development* (5th ed., pp. 553–617). New York: Wiley.

Hirsch, B. J., Roffman, J. G., Deutsch, N. L., Flynn, C. A., Loder, T. L., & Pagano, M. E. (2000). Inner-city youth development organizations: Strengthening programs for adolescent girls. *Journal of Early Adolescence, 20*(2), 210–230.

Horn, T. S. (1987). The influence of teacher-coach behavior on the psychological development of children. In D. Gould & M. R. Weiss (Eds.) *Advances in pediatric sport sciences:* Vol. 2. *Behavioral issues* (pp. 121–142). Champaign, IL: Human Kinetics.

Huebner, A. J. & Mancini, J. A. (2003). Shaping Structured Out-of-School Time Use Among Youth: The Effects of Self, Family, and Friend Systems. *Journal of Youth and Adolescence, 32(6),* 453–463.

Hunt, D. E. (1975). Person–environment interaction: A challenge found wanting before it was tried. *Review of Educational Research, 45,* 209–230.

Jacobs, J. E., Lanza, S., Osgood, D. W., Eccles, J. S., & Wigfield, A. (2002). Changes in children's self-competence and values: Gender and domain differences across grades one through twelve. *Child Development 73*(2), 509–527.

Jacobs, J. E., Vernon, M. K., & Eccles, J. S. (2005). Activity choices in middle childhood: The roles of gender, self-beliefs, and parents' influence. In J. L. Mahoney, R. W. Larson, & J. S. Eccles (Eds.), *Organized activities as contexts of development: Extracurricular activities, after-school and community programs* (pp. 235–254). Mahwah, NJ: Erlbaum.

Jarrett, R. L. (1997). African American family and parenting strategies in impoverished neighborhoods. *Qualitative Sociology, 20,* 275–288.

Jordan, W. J., & Nettles, S. M. (2000). How students invest their time outside of school: Effects on school-related outcomes. *Social Psychology of Education, 3*, 217–243.

Kinney, D. A. (1993). From nerds to normals: The recovery of identity among adolescents from middle school to high schools. *Sociology of Education, 66*, 21–40.

Larson, R. W. (2000). Toward a psychology of positive youth development. *American Psychologist, 55*, 170–183.

Larson, R. W., Hansen, D. M., & Moneta, G. (2006). Differing profiles of developmental experiences across types of organized youth activities. *Developmental Psychology, 42*, 849–863.

Larson, R., Walker, K., & Pearce, N. (2005). Youth-driven and adult-driven youth development programs: Contrasting models of youth–adult relationships. *Journal of Community Psychology, 33*, 57–74.

Lareau, A. (2003). *Unequal childhoods: Class, race, and family life.* Berkeley: University of California Press.

Lauver, S., & Little, P. M. D. (2005). Recruitment and retention strategies for out-of-school time programs. In G. G. Noam (Ed.). H. B. Weiss, P. M. D. Little, and S. M. Bouffard (Issue Eds.). *New Directions for Youth Development. No. 105: Participation in youth programs: Enrollment, attendance, and engagement*, 71–89.

Lauver, S., Little, P. M. D., & Weiss, H. (2004). *Moving beyond the barriers: Attracting and sustaining youth participation in out-of-school time programs.* Retrieved July 27, 2006 from: http://www.gse.harvard.edu/hfrp/content/projects/afterschool/resources/issuebrief6.pdf.

Lerner, R. M. (2006). Developmental science, developmental systems, and contemporary theories of human development. In R. M. Lerner (Ed.), *Handbook of Child Psychology*, Vol. 1: *Theoretical models of human development* (6th ed.). Editors-in-chief: W. Damon & R. M. Lerner. Hoboken, NJ: Wiley and Sons.

Lerner, R. M. (2004). *Liberty: Thriving and civic engagement among America's youth.* Thousand Oaks, CA: Sage Publications.

Loder, T. L. & Hirsch, B. J. (2003). Inner-city youth development organizations: The salience of peer ties among early adolescent girls. *Applied Developmental Science, 7*(1), 2–12.

Luthar, S. S., Shoum, K. A. & Brown, P. J. (2006). Extracurricular Involvement Among Affluent Youth: A Scapegoat for "Ubiquitous Achievement Pressures"?. *Developmental Psychology, 42*(3), 583–597.

Magnusson, D. & Stattin, H. (2006). The person in the environment: Towards a general model for scientific inquiry. In R. M. Lerner (Ed.), *Handbook of Child Psychology*, Vol. 1: *Theoretical models of human development* (6th ed., pp. 400–464). Editors-in-chief: W. Damon & R. M. Lerner. Hoboken, NJ: Wiley.

Magnusson, D. & Stattin, H. (1998). Person-context interaction theories. In W.Damon & R.M. Lerner (Eds.) *Handbook of Child Psychology*, Vol 1: *Theoretical Models of Human Development* (5th ed., pp. 685–759). New York: Wiley.

Mahoney, J. (2000). School extracurricular activity participation as a moderator in the development of antisocial patterns. *Child Development, 71*, 502–516.

Mahoney, J., Larson, R., & Eccles, J. (Eds.). (2005). *Organized activities as contexts of development: Extracurricular activities, after-school and community programs.* Hillsdale, NJ: Lawrence Erlbaum Associates.

Mahoney, J. L., Stattin, H., & Lord, H. (2004). Unstructured youth recreation centre participation and antisocial behaviour development: Selection influences and the moderation role of antisocial peers. *International Journal of Behavioral Development, 28*, 553–560.

Mahoney, J. L., Cairns, B. D., & Farmer, T. W. (2003). Promoting interpersonal competence and educational success through extracurricular activity participation. *Journal of Educational Psychology, 95*, 409–418.

Marsh, H. W., & Kleitman, S. (2002). Extracurricular school activities: The good, the bad, and the nonlinear. *Educational Review, 72*, 464–514.

McHale, S. M., Updegraf, K. A., & Jackson-Newsom, J. (2000). When does parents' differential treatment have negative implications for siblings? *Social Development, 9*, 149–172.

Molnar, B. E., Gortmaker, S. L., Bull, F. C., & Buka, S. L. (2004). Unsafe to play? Neighborhood disorder and lack of safety predict reduced physical activity among urban children and adolescents. *American Journal of Health Promotion, 18(5)*, 378–386.

Mounts, N. S. (2002). Parental management of adolescent peer relationships in context: The role of parenting style. *Journal of Family Psychology, 16*, 1, 58–69.

National Research Council and Institute of Medicine (2002). *Community programs to promote youth development*. Committee on Community-Level Programs for Youth. In J. Eccles & J. A. Gootman (Eds.), Board on Children, Youth, and Families, Division of Behavioral and Social Science and Education. Washington, DC: National Academy Press.

Overton, W. F. (2006). Developmental psychology: Philosophy, concepts, methodology. In R. M. Lerner (Ed.), *Handbook of Child Psychology*, Vol. 1: *Theoretical models of human development* (6th ed., pp. 18–88). Editors-in-chief: W. Damon & R. M. Lerner. Hoboken, NJ: Wiley.

Parke, R. D., Killian, C., Dennis, J., et al., (2003). Managing the external environment: The parent as active agent in the system. In L. Kuczynski (Ed.), *Handbook of dynamic in parent-child relations* (pp. 247–270). Thousand Oaks, CA: Sage.

Parke, R. D., & O'Neil, R. (1999). Social relationships across contexts: Family-peer linkages. In W.A. Collins & B. Laursen (Eds.) *The Minnesota Symposium on Child Psychology: Vol. 30.* Relationships as developmental contexts (pp. 211–239). Mahwah, NJ: Erlbaum.

Pearce, N. J., & Larson, R. W. (2006). How teens become engaged in youth development programs: The process of motivational change in a civic activism organization. *Applied Developmental Science, 10*, 121–131.

Pedersen, S., & Seidman, E. (2005). Contexts and correlates of out-of-school activity participation among low-income urban adolescents. In J. L. Mahoney, R. W. Larson, & J. S. Eccles (Eds.), *Organized activities as contexts of development: Extracurricular activities, after-school and community programs* (pp. 85 – 110). Mahwah, NJ: Erlbaum.

Persson, A., Kerr, M., & Stattin, H. (2007). Staying in or moving away from structured activities: Explanations involving parents and peers. *Developmental Psychology, 43*, 197–207.

Quinn, J. (1999). Where needs meet opportunity: Youth development programs for early teens. In R. Behrman (Ed.), *The future of children: When school is out* (pp. 96–116). Washington, DC: The David and Lucile Packard Foundation.

Quiroz, P. (2000). A comparison of the organizational and cultural contexts of extracurricular participation and sponsorship in two high schools. *Educational Studies, 31*, 249–275.

Roffman, J. G., Suaurez-Orozco, C., & Rhodes, J. (2003). Facilitating positive development in immigrant youth: The role of mentors and community organizations. In F. A. VIllarruel, D. F. Perkins, L. M. Borden, & J. G. Keith (Eds.) *Community youth development: Programs, policies, and practices* (pp. 90–117). Thousand Oaks, CA: Sage.

Rogoff, B. (2003). *The cultural nature of human development.* Oxford: Oxford University Press.

Roth, J. L,, & Brooks-Gunn, J. (2003). Youth development programs: Risk, prevention and policy. *Journal of Adolescent Health, 32*(3), 170–182.

Rural School & Community Trust (2005). Retrieved on January 7, 2008 at http://www.ruraledu.org/site/c.beJMIZOCIrH/b.2820295/

Ryan, R. M., & Deci, E. L. (2000). Self-determination theory and the facilitation of intrinsic motivation, social development, and well-being. *American Psychologist, 55*, 68–78.

Save the Children (2002). *America's forgotten children: Child poverty in rural America.* Retrieved on January 20, 2008 at: http://www.savethechildren.org/publications/

Scanlan, T. K., Babkes, M. L., & Scanlan, L. A. (2005). Participation in sport: A developmental glimpse at emoation. In J. L. Mahoney, R. W. Larson, & J. S. Eccles (Eds.), *Organized activities as contexts of development: Extracurricular activities, after-school and community programs* (pp. 275–310). Mahwah, NJ: Erlbaum.

Seidman, E., & Pedersen, S. (2003). Holistic contextual perspectives on risk, protection, and competence among low-income urban adolescents. In S.S. Luthar (Ed.) *Resilience and vulnerability: Adaption in the context of childhood adversities* (pp. 318–342). Cambridge, England: Cambridge University Press.

Shann, M. H. (2001). Students' use of time outside of school: A case for after school programs for urban middle school youth. *The Urban Review, 33*, 339–356.

Sharp, C., Pocklington, K., & Weindling, D. (2002). Study support and the development of the self-regulated learner. *Educational Research, 44*, 29–41.

Simpkins, S. D., & Becnel, J. N. (2007). *Compromises, consistency, and change in children's time use.* Manuscript submitted for publication.

Simpkins, S. D., Davis-Kean, P. E., & Eccles, J. S. (2005a). Parents' socializing behavior and children's participation in math, science, and computer out-of-school activities. *Applied Developmental Science, 9*, 14–30.

Simpkins, S. D., Ripke, M., Huston, A. C., & Eccles, J. S. (2005b). Predicting participation and outcomes in out-of-school activities: Similarities and differences across social ecologies. In G. G. Noam (Ed.). H. B. Weiss, P. M. D. Little, and S. M. Bouffard (Issue Eds.). *New Directions for Youth Development. No. 105: Participation in youth programs: Enrollment, attendance, and engagement*, 51–70.

Simpkins, S. D., Fredricks, J., Davis-Kean, P., & Eccles, J. S. (2006). Healthy minds, healthy habits: The influence of activity involvement in middle childhood. In

A. C. Huston & M. N. Ripke (Eds.), *Developmental contexts in middle childhood* (pp. 283–302). New York: Cambridge University Press.

Slomkowski, C., Rende, R., Novak, S., et al. (2005). Sibling effects on smoking in adolescence: Evidence for social influence from a genetically informed design. *Addiction, 100,* 430–438.

Storey, P. & Brannen, J. (2000) *Young People and Transport in Rural Areas.* Retrieved November 22, 2007, from: http://www.jrf.org.uk/knowledge/findings/socialpolicy/750.asp

Vandell, D. L, Shumow, L., & Posner, J. (2005). After-school programs for low-income children: Differences in program quality. In J. L. Mahoney, R. W. Larson, & J. S. Eccles (Eds.), *Organized activities as contexts of development: Extracurricular activities, after-school and community programs* (pp. 437–456). Mahwah, NJ: Erlbaum.

Whiteman, S.D., McHale, S. M., & Crouter, A. C. (2007). Explaining sibling similarities: Perceptions of sibling influences. *Journal of Youth and Adolescence, 35,* 963–972.

Wigfield, A. & Eccles, J. S. (2002). Motivational beliefs, values, and goals. *Annual Review of Psychology, 53,* 109–132.

Williams, W. & Lester, N. (2000). Out of control: Parents' becoming violent at youth sporting events. *Sports Illustrated, 93,* 86–95.

Windle, M. (2000). Parental, sibling, and peer influences on adolescent substance use and alcohol problems. *Applied Developmental Science, 4,* 98–110.

Youniss, J., McLellan, J. A., Su, Y., & Yates, M. (1999). The role of community service in identity development: Normative, unconventional, and deviant orientations. *Journal of Adolescent Research, 14,* 2, 248–261.

Zarrett, N. R. (2007). The dynamic relation between out-of-school activities and adolescent development (Doctoral dissertation, University of Michigan, 2006). *Dissertation Abstracts International, 67*(10), 6100B.

Zarrett, N. & Eccles, J. S. (2006). The passage to adulthood: Challenges of late adolescence. In S.Piha and G. Hall (Vol. Eds.) *New Directions for Youth Development. Preparing Youth for the Crossing: From Adolescence to Early Adulthood,* (Issue 111, pp. 13–28). Wiley Periodicals Inc.

Zarrett, N., Peck, S., & Eccles, J. S. (2007, March). What does it take to get youth involved?: A pattern-centered approach for studying youth, family, and community predictors of youth out-of-school activity participation. In A, Bohnert (Chair), *Innovative approaches for assessing adolescents' experiences in organized activities.* Symposium conducted at the biennial meeting of the Society for Research on Child Development, Boston, MA.

Zarrett, N., Peck, S., von Eye, A., & Eccles, J. S. (under review). Do extracurricular activities matter: Addressing the endogeneity issue. Manuscript submitted for publication.

CHAPTER 4

THE EVOLUTION OF TRUST RELATIONSHIPS IN SCHOOL–COMMUNITY PARTNERSHIP DEVELOPMENT

From Calculated Risk-Taking to Unconditional Faith

Catherine M. Hands

This chapter aims to clarify the process of creating school–community partnerships by explicating the role of trust in these relationships from comparative case study data of two secondary schools with numerous partnerships and characterized by economic and cultural diversity. Drawing on the analysis of documents, observations, and 25 interviews with principals, teachers, and community partners, trust and the presence of personal networks are shown to facilitate partnering, from goal-setting through activity selection to ongoing assessment and maintenance. A base level of trust is required to successfully contact potential partners and to negotiate the goals and collaborative activities. This trust grows through repeated interaction where

Promising Practices for Family and Community Involvement during High School, pages 53–69

partners' expectations are met. Partners with a reputation of trustworthiness attract other potential partners in the community, which has implications for school personnel who wish to increase community involvement in their schools. This chapter assists both educators and researchers to better understand the partnership process and to enable educators to effectively establish partnerships with community members.

A growing number of schools and school districts are concluding that collaboration is an avenue through which students' needs may be met and achievement promoted. In economically and culturally diverse societies typical of Canada and the United States, the gap in student achievement between advantaged and disadvantaged groups is widening (Davies, 2002). Schools are finding it increasingly difficult to create educational programs to address the diverse needs of the students (Merz & Furman, 1997). Consequently, some school personnel are looking to garner the financial and material resources, as well as the social support and breadth of educational experiences available in the community to supplement students' in-school learning opportunities in order to meet students' various needs through partnerships (Hands, 2005).

Similarly, and for some time now, a number of educational researchers have been advocating the benefits of partnerships between schools, families, and communities as a means of promoting student achievement for all students (Davies & Johnson, 1996; Epstein & Sanders, 1998; Henderson, 1987; Henderson, Mapp, Johnson, & Davies, 2007). The cultivation of partnerships with community organizations and citizens may be particularly important for secondary school students who are transitioning from school to work or postsecondary institutions in the broader community. Common sentiments regarding the importance of school, of exerting academic effort, of assisting others, and of staying in school may be reinforced by a variety of influences on the students (Epstein, 1995). That said, adolescents who are transitioning from school to work or postsecondary educational institutions can anticipate variations in the occupational and social practices as well as the values systems within the broader society, in comparison to those of their families and those within the school (Hands, 2008). The advantage to community involvement in their schooling is twofold, for it has the potential to enhance students' learning opportunities and to ease the transition from high school.

Given the valuable role that community involvement can play in secondary schooling, the following research question was investigated to yield insight into the process of forming partnerships: *How do educators in secondary schools develop school–community partnerships?* Over the course of interviewing the participants, trust was identified by a number of educators in the schools and their community partners as an important issue in the development of liaisons. Using the qualitative data generated in an in-depth study of two case examples, this chapter highlights the nature and roles of trust involved in the establishment and maintenance of partnerships.

The section that follows is an overview of existing literature to provide a framework for partnering as well as the interactions and levels of trust among individuals establishing liaisons.

THE CONNECTIONS BETWEEN SCHOOLS AND COMMUNITIES

School–community partnerships can be described as the "connections between schools and community individuals, organizations, and businesses that are forged to promote students' social, emotional, physical, and intellectual development" (Sanders, 2001, p. 20). The community may include the for-profit sector such as businesses, the public sector such as educational institutions, government and military organizations, and healthcare facilities, as well as the non-profit sector such as faith organizations, cultural, and recreational facilities in addition to other community-based organizations and individuals in the community (see Epstein, 1995; Hands, 2005; Sanders, 2001; Wohlstetter, Malloy, Smith, & Hentschke, 2003). The "connections," or partnership activities, may have a focus on families, the school, community development, and often, a primary focus on student needs and achievement (Epstein, 2001; Hands, 2005; Sanders, 2001; Sanders & Harvey, 2002). They are characterized by efforts of all parties toward mutually desirable goals that are unattainable in the absence of cooperation (Hargreaves & Fullan, 1998; Keith, 1999).

School Community Partnerships

The partnership process can be depicted as seven distinct stages. In Stages One through Three, potential partners at the school and in the community are sought and contacted based on needs (Hands, 2005; Sanders, 2001). Partnerships are most easily established through existing professional and social personal networks of relationships, and it is advantageous to outline the possible benefits of liaising for potential partners from the first contact (Hands, 2005). During face-to-face meetings, the school personnel and the community members discuss the possibilities for partnering and establish partnership activities in which all parties benefit, in Stages Four through Six (Hands, 2005). The partners assess the success of the activities in meeting their goals in Stage Seven, and communicate their evaluations as feedback to one another in an ongoing manner (Hands, 2005; Sanders,

2001). If necessary, they modify the partnership or the activities to suit their needs over time (Hands, 2005).

The nature of the partnerships that are cultivated varies. In the study presented later in this chapter, for instance, some students developed social networks and occupational skills by setting up and maintaining a church-affiliated conference center for business meetings and events, or making costumes for theater companies, which enabled the organizations to trim costs. Other students prepared for upcoming musical performances by entertaining the residents of a local nursing home. A partnership between a college broadcasting program and a school station with a public radio frequency gave secondary school students access to the college broadcasting resources and the college students had access to the school's radio station. As these examples illustrate, partnerships have a common focus on education and student achievement; however, the partners collaborate to tailor the activities to the particular needs of all participants, utilizing the available human, material, and financial resources.

THE ROLE OF TRUST IN RELATIONSHIP-BUILDING

As with other types of relationships, trust has a fundamental role in the establishment of partnerships. At each stage of the liaising process, there are opportunities to develop, enhance, or diminish trust among partners. In their multidisciplinary review of four decades of literature on trust, Tschannen-Moran and Hoy (2000) have distilled common facets of trust in human relationships. For them, "trust is one party's willingness to be vulnerable to another based on the confidence that the latter part is (a) benevolent, (b) reliable, (c) competent, (d) honest, and (e) open" (Tschannen-Moran & Hoy, 2000, p. 556). These facets are present in varying degrees depending on the nature of the relationship (Hoy & Tschannen-Moran, 1999). Moreover, the expression of trust is dynamic and varies over time and across situations and individuals (Tschannen-Moran & Hoy, 2000).

While there are diverse cultural perspectives regarding the concept of trust (see for example González, Moll & Amanti, 2005; Thompson, 2004), Bottery (2003) has developed a theoretical framework for trust that is helpful in explicating the role of trust in partnership development and maintenance. Bottery's framework forms the basis for the discussion of trust that follows in the next sections. Degrees of trust are conceptualized in a hierarchy or on a continuum that increase in complexity from a cognitive calculation of one's own confidence in others' ability and motivation to do what they say they will do, to a quality of the relationship involving emotional and ethical components (Bottery, 2003; Macmillan, Meyer & Northfield, 2004).

The Essential Elements of Trust

When determining initially whether to trust another, people subjectively assess their vulnerability in a situation using a variety of factors, such as personal predisposition, the amount of information they have regarding a situation, including an understanding of any formal and informal organizational social structures and norms (for example, policies, contracts, legal mandates), the knowledge of a person's past performance, the amount of risk connected with the situation, and the ability to sanction the person for failure to perform the action(s) required of the individual (Gambetta, 1988, Macmillan et al., 2004; Tschannen-Moran & Hoy, 2000). The probability that another person will carry out a prescribed action independent of monitoring determines whether the person is predictable and to be trusted (Bottery, 2003; Gambetta, 1988; O'Hara, 2004). This constitutes calculative trust (Bottery, 2003; Tschannen-Moran & Hoy, 2000).

Practice Trust

Performance-related trust is a greater level of trust involving calculative, ethical, and emotional characteristics. It is developed with repeated interaction (Bottery, 2003). This knowledge-based trust enables individuals to more accurately predict others' reliability in familiar situations (Macmillan et al., 2004; Tschannen-Moran & Hoy, 2000). For example, Macmillan and colleagues (2004) found that through the observation of administrators' behaviors across many different situations, their underlying values systems could then be inferred by others. Research on networked learning communities finds that working and reflecting together on a common focus can build social trust and respect (Bryk, Camburn, & Louis, 1999; Earl, Katz, Elgie, Ben Jaafar, & Foster, 2006). This type of trust relationship is esteemed for more than information or resources, for it is valued in its own right (Bottery, 2003) and can withstand unmet expectations especially if those involved work to restore good faith (Tschannen-Moran & Hoy, 2000).

Trust in the Profession

Role trust builds on practice trust because it formally emphasizes the ethical aspects of individuals' behavior and relationships with one another (Bottery, 2003). The values that are inculcated within a profession or an organization are transmitted to the individuals upon their entrance into the profession or organization (Bottery, 2003; Tschannen-Moran & Hoy, 2000). This code of ethics guides the individuals' future actions, and enables assumptions and predictions to be made by others regarding the nature of the individuals' actions. It encompasses a formal ethical code characteristic of an occupation (such as medicine) that grounds behaviors (Bottery, 2003), as well as the legal policies and mandates that govern individuals' professional actions (Macmillan et al., 2004), and the informal social structures such as the culture and learned behavior patterns characteristic of the organization (Tschannen-Moran & Hoy, 2000).

Associative Trust

The most complex level of trust entails an interpersonal relationship that is akin to the trust between friends (Macmillan et al., 2004). It incorporates personal thoughts, feelings, shared values, and ideals (Sergiovanni, 1994; Stefkovich & Shapiro, 2002), and goes beyond trust in the profession (Bottery, 2003, Macmillan et al., 2004). In unconditional trust relationships, the parties identify with one another such that there is empathy with the other's desires and intentions and an understanding that each party can effectively act on behalf of one another (Tschannen-Moran & Hoy, 2000). Here, participants in the relationship share an implicit trust without assessing others' trustworthiness, requiring additional information about the situation or the other person(s), or referring to professional role expectations (Bottery, 2003; Macmillan et al., 2004).

This is the level of trust noted in school reform literature on networked learning communities that enables individuals to work together toward common goals even when they have different opinions and approaches to building knowledge (Lieberman & Grolnick, 1996). Moreover, it enables them to work independently as well as to collaborate with others in the group to further the network's shared focus (Earl et al., 2006).

Philosophies of Human Nature

Several additional types of trust mediate the development of the trust relationships previously mentioned, and influence the degree of trust among parties (Tschannen-Moran & Hoy, 2000). Research from the field of social psychology suggests that individuals have implicit theories or philosophies about humankind (Bruner & Tagiuri, 1954; Wrightsman, 1964). For example, people vary from one another in terms of the extent to which they believe people to be trustworthy or untrustworthy (Wrightsman, 1964). As Tschannen-Moran and Hoy (2000) note, "certain people have an attitude that makes them inclined to extend trust more readily" (p. 559). Bottery (2003) refers to this as existential trust. He states that existential trust is based on "the individual's confidence in the rightness of the world" (p. 256), that needs to be believed if the individual is going to cultivate trust relationships.

Bottery (2003) builds on this notion by conceptualizing that these personal philosophies are affected by *meso* and *macro* trust. This is the belief individuals have in their organization's appointed leader, and more importantly, the overall organizational cultures or philosophies within which they work (meso level), as well as the level of trust people have in individuals (in particular, public figures such as politicians) within the broader society in general (macro level). These aspects of trust serve to inform people's views of life (Bottery, 2003).

METHODOLOGY

A qualitative case study of two secondary schools in a southern Ontario school board with a reputation for establishing strong partnerships and numerous collaborative activities with community members was used to examine school–community partnership development experiences. Pseudonyms were used for all places and individuals in order to protect the anonymity of the study participants. Blackpool High School, which was located in the low socio-economic, culturally homogeneous town and surrounding rural community of Queenstown, and Manchester Secondary School, which was situated within the multicultural, suburban, low- to middle-income community of Beaconsville, were selected. Both schools had cultivated between 75 and 80 school–community liaisons.

During the data collection process, 25 interviews were conducted with the principals, teachers, and school support staff during three site visits at Manchester and four site visits at Blackpool, as well as with members of the community who were involved in partnership activities with the schools (such as individual community citizens, and contact people for businesses, government offices, senior citizens' organizations, and health care institutions). A snowball technique (Merriam, 1998) was used to obtain community participants for the study. During interviews with school personnel, the names and contact information of the community partners with whom they had the strongest relationships were requested. Most interviews were individually conducted; however, two focus groups were conducted to accommodate the schedules of the participants.

In total, the 30 individuals participating in the study were involved in one semi-structured, open-ended interview of approximately 45 minutes in length that was transcribed verbatim. Additionally, observations were conducted at the schools and documents that were pertinent to the partnership activities, including the schools' mission statements, memos, school plans and meeting minutes, were gathered from school staff and community partners. Multiple sources of data were sought to establish construct-validity through the triangulation of the data (Merriam, 1998; Rothe, 2000; Yin, 1994).

The collected data were coded and analyzed, and incidents were compared across the data (Bogdan & Biklen, 1982; Merriam, 1998) for emerging categories and themes. The constant comparative method enabled new categories and themes to be developed and existing ones to be evaluated and modified. Once the within-case analysis was completed, the cross-case analysis (Merriam, 1998; Miles & Huberman, 1994) was conducted to yield the categories which emerged across the data from Manchester and Blackpool. Thus, an examination of the partnership practices of the school administrator, teacher, support staff, and community member participants at both schools facilitated an investigation of similarities and differences between the partnership-initiating techniques used and the influences on their successful development.

ANALYSIS AND DISCUSSION

Many of the participants in this study noted that trust was an essential element in the partnership process from the beginning of the relationship. In this section, the various roles that trust played in two high school–community partnerships are illustrated.

The Establishment of Trust in the Early Stages of Partnering

For both educators and community members, communication was considered key to developing trust between partners. During initial conversations, potential partners outlined exactly what was desired from the liaisons and the involved individuals. Blackpool's Community-based Education Department head, Al, stated that "the 'how' is the difficult part...[I]t's networking, it's trust, it's honesty, it's being upfront with them to begin with exactly what they're going to get." Community partners at both schools said that clear expectations were essential for the partnership activities and the individuals involved. They also identified the importance of promising only what was within their means to deliver.

After initial conversations, levels of trust were determined and the potential for partnering was assessed. Manchester's Community-based Education head, Kevin, said,

> I ask myself... after I've been to a cold call is, "What is my gut feeling? Are they looking for free labor? Or are they willing to engage in learning?" And if my gut feeling tells me this particular work placement just wants a worker, I won't... carry on that relationship.

The same was true for the community partners. For example, a Queenstown physician accepted Blackpool students for work placements at his office only after personally interviewing potential student participants and outlining clear expectations. This determination of a working level of trust was necessary to engage in partnership activities with the other individual(s).

These findings highlight the key role of two-way communication and the establishment of reliability and dependability in developing trust, which are consistent with existing findings (see Tschannen-Moran & Hoy, 2000). Several study participants noted that schools and citizens attracted potential partners because they had established good reputations and the positive results of their work were known within the community. Regardless, it seems necessary for potential partners to have personal, face-to-face conversations before they gauge their levels of trust and make predictions of others' future behavior in a school–community partnership.

If a base level of trust among partners was established, collaborative activities were developed. Several community partners in particular noted the importance of school personnel and other citizens being open to others' suggestions for the liaisons. As one Blackpool community partner stated about a partnership, "you need to keep an eye on it, but you need to let people run with it also.... You've got to have faith in the partnerships that you've developed and let them run with their ideas too." This served to demonstrate respect for others' ideas as well as trust in their capacity to engage in the collaborative activities.

These findings support the notion that partnerships not only need a base level of trust in order to be initially established, but in order to grow, they need tangible demonstrations of trust among the partners from the beginning of the relationship. This lends credence to Bottery's (2003) claim that being trusted is an important aspect of a trust relationship.

Community Members' Personal Philosophies Influence Their Willingness to Partner

Once initial contact was established, more often than not, partnerships were developed. Typically, school personnel had little difficulty engaging community members in liaisons. Often, these community members had personal philosophies of human nature that were conducive to establishing trust relationships with others.

All but two of the community partners stated that they participated in partnerships for personal reasons. Some citizens enjoyed working with adolescents. One Blackpool partner observed that young people are refreshingly positive about life and the world in which they live. Two citizens who participated in this study agreed to partner with school personnel because they were parents, and thus had a desire to assist youth and to promote their growth and development.

Several other community partners observed that a social conscience spurs many people to help students and other citizens. As a business owner and Blackpool partner, Dan, commented, "[I]t depends on the type of humanitarian you are." For example, a church-affiliated conference center director emphasized the value of all persons:

> Sometimes we get kids who feel they're worth nothing... I feel we, as a Christian church and a Christian organization, need to be involved... with giving these young people a sense of self-worth. We know these young people are worthy.... [T]hey need people around them, who show we care about them.

The president of an international media corporation and Manchester partner noted that it was essential to assist people who make their needs known. For these and other community partners, their belief in the goodness and generosity of others provided them with the motivation to partner with schools. Further, this motivation was the foundation of trust necessary to engage in partnership activities involving people with whom they had not previously established a relationship. This supports Bottery's (2003) notion that existential trust influences the base level of trust necessary for establishing partnerships.

A Shortcut to Creating Partnerships

Some partnerships in this study began as social relationships. For all of those interviewed for this study, partnerships were most easily established among individuals who had existing relationships. At Manchester, the principal had an existing friendship with the media company president. Like the principal and his wife, the president's wife was an educator and their children went to the same school. At a social event, they established a partnership which entailed a monetary donation to the school's radio station and work with the students designed to discourage them from engaging in music piracy.

For a senior citizens' club and Blackpool school council community representative said:

> I taught [for] years at the high school... The principal, Monica Kenny, was in [my] department that we had in the '70s and '80s... With the school council, Monica asked me if I would sit on it... [T]hey'll sometimes ask me if I know of anybody who can help with an item... because I have contacts with people in the community.

Previously established personal or collegial connections, then, paved the way for developing partnership activities. Participants reported establishing most of their partnerships through people with whom they were already associated. Associative trust plays a role here. Potential partners have shared values and interests, an understanding of the others' attitudes and behaviors and a relationship that incorporates an affective element (Bottery, 2003). This level of trust is conducive to establishing a relationship without further assessment of the others' trustworthiness and the likelihood that they would act in an agreed-upon manner (Bottery, 2003; Macmillan et al., 2004; Tschannen-Moran & Hoy, 2000).

Trust by Proxy

In many circumstances, the participants effectively established partnerships from personal associations; however, they reported that they utilized others' networks for this purpose as well. Some of the partnerships reported in this study were developed with people who were associates of relatives, friends, and colleagues. For example, a Blackpool community partner and costume-maker became involved with several partnerships because her husband was a teacher at the school. As a result of her community connections, the costume-maker engaged Family Studies students in costume-making for two theaters. As this example illustrates, the individuals do not necessarily have to have an existing trust relationship to successfully develop the collaborative activities. Rather, they acquire an initial understanding of the others' character and reliability from someone they trust.

This type of trust differs from others previously discussed. Proxy trust does not require tangible evidence of the others' adherence to formal and informal guiding principles for behavior. Indeed, most of the participants in this study did not have a formal professional code of behavior or ethics. This illustrates that trust can be conferred on other individuals in the absence of any personal knowledge of the others' abilities, values, and motivations. Regardless, it is necessary for the individuals to "prove" themselves once the partnerships are established. One Blackpool partner and civil servant observed:

> There's nothing like a personal recommendation from a person you trust and know. Provided that... the person is good.... [Someone] can have all the associations in the world, but if the person is not a good worker, then that's no good.

Building Trust and the Maintenance of Partnerships

The teachers and community members noted that it was easier to partner with people who are predictable, who have commonalities, and who have a known agenda. This is consistent with Tschannen-Moran and Hoy's (2000) findings, in which they noted that trust judgments are based in part on assumed shared values. They found that people tend to more easily trust others they think are similar to themselves. Indeed, they and other scholars have noted that distrust develops in an organization when individuals are perceived as not sharing fundamental cultural values (Sitkin & Roth, 1993; Tschannen-Moran & Hoy, 2000).

The Facilitators of Trust Development

Assumptions of another individual's values, attitudes and possibly, predictions of his or her behaviors, can be made based on personal aspects as seemingly inconsequential as appearance or attire. Al noted that when he went to visit partners in the community, he dressed to blend in with the work culture. Dressing in a similar fashion contributed to others' perceptions of the commonalities between themselves and Al, which served to build trust among the partners.

When looking to establish partnerships, the participants in this study conducted face-to-face meetings to establish common ground, and the possibilities for partnering activities. For example, Manchester Guidance department head, Susan, and the college broadcasting program coordinator, Chris, who partnered with the school, held informal meetings that also involved Manchester's principal and the communications teacher. In talking about the establishment of the partnership, Chris recollected:

> The meetings... were... partly filled with... faculty and people talking about their great experiences teaching kids, and I think that that was a commonality that started the... conversation, so I think that [establishing the partnership] was not very difficult *at all.*

All of the meeting participants were educators, either at the secondary school or at the college-level, with an interest in students and their achievement. They used this common reference point to build a partnership that was beneficial to students at both the school and college. This example as well as the meetings between the other study participants may be considered a form of performance-related practice trust. Additionally, this partnership, as well as the four involving healthcare professionals and the partnership engaging the church official, may also be seen to incorporate role trust. There was an initial base level of trust present prior to the meetings and an interest in partnering with the others involved. The commonalities that came to the forefront served to deepen the trust between the partners in a manner similar to that among the individuals working in networked learning communities, due to their shared foci and interests (Bryk et al., 1999; Earl et al., 2006).

The Nurturing of Trust

Once established, the reliable performances of those involved toward agreed-upon goals increased the likelihood that the study respondents would continue to participate in their existing partnerships. The family physician and Blackpool partner observed:

> If the first student I had . . . had come in late, and showed up dressed inappropriately, and . . . was a negative influence in the office, well then I probably wouldn't take anybody back. . . . If you get one [student who doesn't perform to expectations] and it's your seventh or something, you can always sort of say, "Well, you know, this didn't work, but that's okay, we can try again.

In order to minimize the possibility of partnership termination, the partners' ability to meet the goals of the collaborative activities is essential, according to all study participants. These resulting trusting relationships may serve to build macro trust in the participants for other individuals, as described by Bottery (2003). This may lead to a greater overall trust in other people (Wrightsman, 1964) and the likelihood that the study participants and other individuals in the community would be receptive to other collaborative ventures with other people in the future.

Poor performance constituted a misuse of trust and without existing practice trust, resulted in a subsequent decrease in levels of trust between partners (see Gambetta, 1988; Tschannen-Moran & Hoy, 2000). Through coaching the students to ensure that they understood that their behavior had a direct impact on the existence of the relationships, and by providing support for the community partners and the partnership activities, both Al and Kevin were able to maintain the partnerships over time. Further, these educators claimed that their community partners trusted them to send "good" students to participate in the activities. Both the students and the educators demonstrated their dependability over repeated encounters (Bottery, 2003) and they had a reputation for being trustworthy (Coleman, 1988; Tschannen-Moran & Hoy, 2000).

From the community partners' perspective, it was equally necessary to ensure that their partners trusted them to perform agreed-upon collaborative activities. On occasion, some partnership activities needed to end before one party lived up to the terms of the agreement. If that happened, clear communication was necessary to explain the circumstances and to maintain the relationship, according to the public health nurse and the director of a child and youth social services organization who had social workers engaged with the students at both schools.

Thus, it was crucial for all participants in the activities to perform in an agreed-upon manner in order to maintain the relationships and to build practice trust between the partners. Inability to do so resulted in a loss of trust among partners unless steps were taken to communicate the reasons behind non-performance of the relationships' goals. The participants' experiences demonstrate that "a self-reinforcing pattern of trust emerges as repeated cycles of exchange, risk-taking, and successful fulfillment of expectations strengthen the willingness of trusting parties to rely upon each other" (Tschannen-Moran & Hoy, 2000, p. 562).

CONCLUSIONS

As with other relationships, trust plays an integral role in the establishment and maintenance of partnerships. A basic level of trust was needed to successfully contact potential partners and to negotiate the goals and collaborative activities of the partnerships. This trust was mediated by individuals' philosophies of human nature regarding the trustworthiness of other people, and their confidence in the integrity and justice of the society in which they live (Bottery, 2003; Tschannen-Moran & Hoy, 2000). For the participants in this study, collaborative activities were easier to negotiate among people with whom there was an existing trust relationship. In these situations, the partners already had an understanding of the others' values and actions and an emotional component to their relationships (Bottery, 2003; Macmillan et al., 2004) which expedited the partnership development. In some cases, trust in potential partners was conferred as a result of the trust the participants had in their friends and professional colleagues, which builds on the existing trust frameworks. Once the partnerships were established, successful engagement in the collaborative activities over time built performance trust (Bottery, 2003; Macmillan, 2004; Tschannen-Moran & Hoy, 2000) and facilitated the maintenance of these relationships.

For certain, partnerships take work on the parts of those involved in order to build trust and maintain the relationships; however, the benefits to be realized are substantial. The partnerships in this study not only provided students with academic support and learning opportunities with the financial, material, and human resources in the community, but there were additional benefits of partnering beyond those envisioned by the principals and their faculty. The schools garnered additional resources and public support from the board and the community because of their profiles in the community. The partnerships expanded the students' networks and increased their social capital, consistent with Mawhinney's (2002) findings. By interacting with citizens in their community, the students had opportunities to establish trustworthiness, they built relationships with others in the environment and they enhanced their knowledge base through access to information, learning and occupational experiences (Coleman, 1988; Coleman & Hoffer, 1987). As a result, a number of community partners and several teachers noted that the students successfully gained employment with the community partners following the students' involvement in the collaborative activities.

Moreover, partnerships promote a renewed focus on civics and citizenship among the students. Many of the liaisons in this study encouraged the students to adopt outward-looking perspectives. Thus the partnering practices in this study promoted students' acquisition of "the knowledge, skills and attitudes necessary to function effectively as citizens in a democracy" (Westheimer & Kahne, 2002, p. 14). These findings suggest, then, that partnering with community members is an avenue through which school personnel may gain access to a variety of resources in the community that they do not have within the school. For the participants in this study, the benefits for the students made it worth the effort it took to cultivate and nurture the trust needed to fuel the partnerships.

REFERENCES

Bogdan, R. C., & Biklen, S. K. (1982). *Qualitative research for education: An introduction to theory and methods.* Boston: Allyn & Bacon.

Bottery, M. (2003). The management and mismanagement of trust. *Educational Management & Administration,* 31(3), 245–261. [Electronic version.]

Bruner, J. S., & Tagiuri, R. (1954). The perception of people. In G. Lindzey (Ed.), *Handbook of social psychology* (pp. 634–654). Reading, MA: Addison-Wesley.

Bryk, A., Camburn, E., & Louis, K. S. (1999). Professional community in Chicago elementary schools: facilitating factors and organizational consequences. *Educational Administration Quarterly, 35,* Supplement, 751–781.

Coleman, J. S. (1988). Social capital in the creation of human capital. *American Journal of Sociology, 94,* Supplement, S95–S120.

Coleman, J. S., & Hoffer, T. (1987). *Public and private high schools: The impact of communities.* New York: Basic Books, Inc.

Davies, D. (2002). The 10th school revisited: Are school/family/community partnerships on the reform agenda now? *Phi Delta Kappan, 83*(5), 388–392.

Davies, D., & Johnson, V. R. (Eds.). (1996). Crossing boundaries: Family, community, and school partnerships. *International Journal of Educational Research, 25*(1), Special Issue.

Earl, L., Katz, S., Elgie, S, Ben Jaafar, S., & Foster, L. (2006, May). How networked learning communities work: Volume 1 The Report. Report prepared for the National College of School Leadership Networked Learning Communities Programme.

Epstein, J. L. (1995). School/family/community partnerships: Caring for the children we share. *Phi Delta Kappan, 76*(9), 701–712.

Epstein, J. L. (2001). *School, family, and community partnerships: Preparing educators and improving schools.* Boulder, CO: Westview Press.

Epstein, J. L., & Sanders, M. G. (1998). What we learn from international studies of school-family-community partnerships. *Childhood Education, 74*(6), 392–394.

Gambetta, D. (1988). Can we trust trust? In D. Gambetta (Ed.), *Trust: Making and breaking cooperative relations* (pp. 213–219). Oxford: Basil Blackwell.

González, N., Moll, L. C., & Amanti, C. (2005). Introduction: Theorizing practices. In N. González, L. C. Moll, & C. Amanti (Eds.), *Funds of knowledge: Theorizing practices in households, communities, and classrooms* (pp. 1–24). Mahwah, NJ: Lawrence Erlbaum Associates.

Hands, C. (2005). It's who you know and what you know: The process of creating partnerships between schools and communities. *The School Community Journal, 15*(2), 63–84.

Hands, C. M. (2008). Circles of influence: The role of school –community partnerships in character formation and citizenship of secondary school students. *The Alberta Journal of Educational Research, 54*(1), 50–64.

Hargreaves, A., & Fullan, M. (1998). *What's worth fighting for out there?* New York: Teachers College Press.

Henderson, A. (1987). *The evidence continues to grow: Parental involvement improves student achievement.* Columbia, MO: National Committee for Citizens in Education.

Henderson, A. T., Mapp, K. L., Johnson, V. R., & Davies, D. (2007). Beyond the bake sale: The essential guide to family–school partnerships. New York: The New Press.

Hoy, W. K., & Tschannen-Moran, M. (1999). Five faces of trust: An empirical confirmation in urban elementary schools. *Journal of School Leadership, 9,* 184–208.

Keith, N. Z. (1999). Whose community schools? New discourses, old patterns. *Theory Into Practice, 38*(4), 225–234.

Lieberman, A., & Grolnick, M. (1996). Networks and reform in American education. *Teachers College Record, 98*(1), 7–45.

Macmillan, R. B., Meyer, M. J., & Northfield, S. (2004). Trust and its role in principal succession: A preliminary examination of a continuum of trust. *Leadership and Policy in Schools, 3*(4), 275–294. [Electronic version.]

Mawhinney, H. B. (2002). The microecology of social capital formation: Developing community beyond the schoolhouse door. In G. Furman (Ed.), *School as community: From promise to practice* (pp. 235–255). Albany, NY: State University of New York Press.

Merriam, S. B. (1998). *Qualitative research and case study applications in education.* San Francisco: Jossey-Bass.

Merz, C., & Furman, G. (1997). *Community and schools: Promise and paradox.* New York: Teachers College Press.

Miles, M. B., & Huberman, A. M. (1994). *Qualitative data analysis: An expanded sourcebook* (2nd ed.). Thousand Oaks, CA: Sage.

O'Hara, K. (2004). *Trust: From Socrates to spin.* Cambridge, UK: Icon Books.

Rothe, J. P. (2000). *Undertaking qualitative research.* Edmonton, Canada: The University of Alberta Press.

Sanders, M. G. (2001). The role of "community" in comprehensive school, family, and community programs. *The Elementary School Journal, 102*(1), 19–34.

Sanders, M. G., & Harvey, A. (2002). Beyond the school walls: A case study of principal leadership for school–community collaboration. *Teachers College Record, 104*(7), 1345–1368.

Sergiovanni, T. J. (1994). *Building community schools.* San Francisco: Jossey-Bass.

Sitkin, S. B., & Roth, N. L. (1993). Explaining the limited effectiveness of legalistic "remedies" for trust/distrust. *Organizational Science, 4,* 367–392.

Stefkovich, J., & Shapiro, J. P. (2002). Deconstructing communities: Educational leaders and their ethical decision-making processes. In P.T. Begley, & O. Johansson (Eds.), *The ethical dimensions of school leadership* (pp. 77–87). Dordrecht, The Netherlands: Kluwer Academic Publishers.

Thompson, A. (2004). Caring and colortalk: Childhood innocence in White and Black. In V. Siddle Walker & J. R. Snarey (Eds.), *Race-ing moral formation: African American perspectives on care and justice* (pp. 23–37). New York: Teachers College Press.

Tschannen-Moran, M., & Hoy, W. K. (2000). A multidisciplinary analysis of the nature, meaning, and measurement of trust. *Review of Educational Research, 70*(4), 547–593.

Westheimer, J., & Kahne, J. (2002). Education for action: Preparing youth for participatory democracy. In R. Hayduk, & K. Mattson (Eds.), *Democracy's moment: Reforming the American political system for the 21st century* (pp. 91–107). Lanham, MD: Rowman & Littlefield. Retrieved October 8, 2004 from http://www.democraticdialogue.com/DDpdfs/EducationForAction.pdf

Wohlstetter, P., Malloy, C. L., Smith, J., & Hentschke, G. (2003). Cross-sectorial alliances in education: A new approach to enhancing school capacity. (Working paper). Los Angeles: University of Southern California, Rossier School of Education, Center on Educational Governance.

Wrightsman, L. S. (1964). Measurement of philosophies of human nature. *Psychological Reports, 14,* 743–751.

Yin, R. K. (1994). *Case study research: Design and methods* (2nd ed.). Thousand Oaks, CA: Sage Publications.

SECTION TWO

PERSPECTIVES FROM PRACTICE AND POLICY

CHAPTER 5

TRANSITION TO HIGH SCHOOL

Creating Community

Joan Lampert

The transition to high school is a challenge for both students and their parents. This chapter presents background on the transition to high school and a description of the ways in which one Midwestern, suburban high school has addressed concerns regarding the transition of eighth grade students into and though their freshman year. The chapter will focus on a Freshman Advisory program specifically developed for ninth grade students with the mission of helping the freshmen to "Be Well and Do Well," as well as on a Family Center outreach program whose mission is to engage parents and the community by offering classes, workshops, presentations, and discussions on topics relevant both to the community and to the school.

Learning and Development

Currently, developmentalists support the notion that development is bidirectional, occurring within, between, and among physical (both internal

Promising Practices for Family and Community Involvement during High School, pages 73–87

and external, social, cognitive, and emotional systems of human experience (Brofenbrenner & Morris, 1998). The practice of teaching and learning, draws from this nested and complex understanding of development. Kurt Fischer's research strongly suggests that learning occurs across multiple systems at the cellular and brain systems levels (2006). Recent research indicates that the brain experiences a period of synaptic bloom and pruning during adolescence that results in newer, more complex neural systems. This highlights the critical importance of carefully designing environments for adolescents. At the macro-level, the Yale School Development Program developed by James Comer and his colleagues at the Yale Child Study Center (2004) requires staff to approach teaching and learning across six developmental pathways (Joyner, Comer & Ben-Avie, 2004). The pathways panel includes: physical, ethical, social, cognitive, psychological,and language domains. Furthermore, this model requires the school staff to situate themselves firmly within the community they are serving to "develop bonds necessary for effective teaching and learning" (Joyner et al., 2004, p. 22).

School Transitions

Learning, however, is not just an internal issue. It occurs, as well, within a system of education that involves events and conditions that are imposed upon the learner. Of particular interest to this volume are the transitions that occur from middle or junior high to high school. Recent research suggest that younger adolescents, in particular, are less able to navigate transitions. First, they lack the cognitive functions to adequately mange the change. Second, high schools differ significantly from middle schools (Eccles, 2004; Mizelle, 1999; Mizelle & Irwin, 2005). High schools tend to be large and impersonal; require interaction with multiple teachers and staff; rely upon competition rather than cooperation; and rank and track students. Eccles (2004) maintains that transition are developmentally problematic for young adolescents.

There is mounting evidence that the ninth grade transition from eighth to tenth grade is particularly troublesome. Wheelock & Miao (2005) report an expanding ninth grade bulge in which there are significantly more students in ninth grade that there are in eighth or tenth grade—suggesting that students remain in ninth grade for more than one year because they have failed to pass the requisite number of classes to move on the tenth grade. It has been suggested that the presence of even one F in a core semester subject in ninth grade reduces the probability of remaining in school through graduation. University of Michigan Youth Behavior Studies of Alcohol, Tobacco, and other Drug abuse have long found that the transition into high school is correlated with increased substance use and that younger adolescents are more likely than older adolescents to engage in risky behaviors during the after school hours— this in part because they can't work and they don't drive.

DOING WELL AND BEING WELL: EASING THE TRANSITION TO MAINE EAST HIGH SCHOOL

At the level of practice, the vast majority of high school administrators and faculty are concerned with the well-being of incoming freshmen. Maine East High School, a large (2000 students, 300 staff), highly diverse (70% bilingual in one of 57 languages, 40% born overseas, 33% free and reduced-lunch program) school located in the northwest suburbs of Chicago, is no exception.

Four issues strongly suggested our freshmen were challenged by the transition from elementary/junior high to high school. These issues were achievement, attachment, awareness, and attendance. Administrators and staff noted that 37% of the freshmen were failing one or more classes during the first semester. Fewer than 60% of all freshmen were involved with an extracurricular program over the course of their first year in school even though 75 clubs and organizations, as well as fine arts and an extensive sports program were offered. There has been an ongoing perception and concern that a disproportionate number of students have diagnosable psychological disorders, substance abuse problems, and gang involvement. Referrals to social workers, psychologists, and special education seemed to peak in ninth grade. Although some of the referrals were for students who had exhibited some behavioral/emotional concerns in the junior high, many of the referrals were for students who had managed the lower level reasonably well, but had not managed the transition to the high school in the same manner. Furthermore, the administration had been concerned about the number of tardiness, cuts, absences, and the concomitant number of in-school and out-of-school suspensions.

The Freshman Advisory Program

Developing the Program

The most compelling issues identified by the Maine East principal were achievement and attachment. These would become the measures of "success" of the program. Attendance and awareness issues were to be subsumed into the program as part of the curriculum.

A planning committee, consisting of parents, students, administrators, teachers, counselors, and union leaders met for two years to address the transition to ninth grade. During that time, committee members visited nearby programs, researched other programs, and developed an initial curriculum that would be implemented in the fall of 2001. The Advisory at Maine East was developed by blending the components and structure of several models of existing advisories.

Adult Developed and Led Activities

Some advisory models were both developed and led by adults. These typically focused on academics and relied on "outside-in" strategies such as—curriculum mapping and articulation; before and after school activities and looping; small schools and smaller learning communities; as well as a "seminar" period where study skills were taught and tutoring was available. We visited to learn about and were influenced by nearby programs at Rolling Meadows High School and Evanston High School

Adult Developed and Student Led Activities

Other advisory models were developed by adults and led by students. Those typically focused on social issues such as Big-Brother–Big Sister programs; sending the middle school students to the high school to shadow students; peer mediation; and peer mentors who would meet with a small cluster of incoming students one to two times a month either during the first semester or throughout the year. We had visited the program at Stevenson High School in which upper class mentors are paired with freshmen during a 20 minute period opposite a 20 minute lunch and wanted to include a similar component.

Adult and Student Developed/Student Led Activities

In order to meet the mission of "Being Well and Doing Well," approximately 75 % of the freshman class have been assigned to Freshman Advisory; the remaining 25 % participate in other programs designed to meet specific needs (such as ESL newcomers, Title One Academy, honors/gifted, or special education programs). The Advisory program is adult and student developed and student led. In order to address our mission, it was decided that the Advisory would consist of a daily 43 minute period with a full year curriculum. Three days of the week are devoted to tutoring and two days of the week are used to focus on the curriculum initiative. Each month, the advisory staff receives a curriculum book consisting of the calendar for that month, the month's initiatives as well as instructions for the presentation and debriefing of all initiatives for the month. Currently there are 12 sections scheduled throughout the school day with 13 faculty supervisors, 33 mentors and 300 freshmen. Freshman Advisory is facilitated by a half-time coordinator.

Connection with School-wide Faculty

A considerable amount of energy has gone into promoting collaboration between the advisory program and the freshman faculty and into supporting the work in the classroom directly. Whenever possible, the curriculum books also contain a listing of assignments, projects, and critical test dates for Math, Science, History, and English. Furthermore, the calendar also highlights social and cocurricular events such as Homecoming, Fine Arts plays, musicals and exhibits, and sporting events.

The Advisory provides the opportunity for those students who are struggling in a particular subject to meet with faculty for further support. The school provides a Math Resource lab as well as a Writing Lab each period so that students have ready access to those supportive faculty members. Following an orientation to the Library Resource Center, students may use Advisory time to complete projects and do research. Also, because it is a full period, the Advisory provides an opportunity for students to complete make up tests.Finally, counselors take advantage of the Advisory period to connect with their freshmen, and to provide them with information about planning for their four years in high school.

Overview of the Advisory Curriculum

The curriculum for the Advisory consists of two integrated domains. An overview can be seen in Table 5.1. The first relates to those initiatives that support the affective mission of *Being Well* during the transition to high school. The second part of the Advisory curriculum relates to those initiatives that support the academic mission of *Doing Well* during the transition to high school. Throughout the freshman year, students receive academic report cards every four weeks. The Advisory teacher reviews these reports with the students individually. Those students who are having a particularly difficult time are referred to the counseling division for follow-up with their counselors, and if needed with social workers and/or psychologists.

The Family Center: Connection with Larger Community

Another program at Maine East supports the transition to high school (among other goals) by reaching out to the parents through a variety of classes, workshops, and programs. As noted previously, many of the parents of the school's students are immigrants. The parents tend to work multiple jobs and have limited English language skills. It is difficult to engage the parents, not because they don't wish to be involved, but because they have difficulty with the timing of school events and even understanding the ways American schools function.

TABLE 5.1 Overview of Advisory Curriculum

Quarter	Affective Initiatives	Academic Initiatives
First	Becoming a High School Student: Ice breaker activities to create a cohesive group identity.	Becoming a High School Student: Set academic goals, learn study skills adapted for the high school, track their grades weekly through the student/parent portal, receive academic support from mentors and encouragement to use peer tutoring and subject area resource labs.
Second	Understanding and Reconciling Conflict: Participate in activities based upon Balanced and Restorative Justice to understand the effects of conflict to the individuals involved and to the group as a whole; explore the long term effects of cyber-bullying.	Preparation for Finals: Test Questions from the Core courses rehearsed and reviewed, general test taking, study skills, and stress management skills taught.
Third	Community Service: Freshman creates his/her own quilt square designed to convey a personal meaning of "peace" to be pieced, stitched and tied into a crib sized quilt that is given to a child living in a shelter program for battered women.	Preparation for State Testing: Freshmen take their first levels of state testing. The advisory curriculum focuses on the value and importance of the tests, test strategies, and types of questions that typically appear on the tests.
Fourth	Increasing Self Awareness and Self Care: Suicide/Depression Prevention workshop (coincides with reading of Romeo and Juliet); examination of popular media leading to discussion about eating disorders and dating violence: study drugs and alcohol as they make plans for a healthy summer and transition into 10th grade.	Preparation for Finals: focuses on staying the course to the end of school and preparation for finals. Goals are discussed for finals, study maps are planned and review questions are again gathered and presented from the core courses.

The Family Center is a collaborative outreach program specifically developed to connect with the parents and families of the student body. The program was created in response to the increasing numbers of immigrant families who enroll their children at Maine East and who, due to language and culture, may feel disconnected from the "culture" of an American high school. Using guidelines set by Epstein (2002) and her colleagues at Johns Hopkins' National Network of Partnership Schools, the Family Center currently is focused on creating initiatives that reflect three types of parent involvement

- Collaborating with the Community: coordinating resources and services from the community for families, students, and the schools, and provide services to the community
- Parenting: assisting families with parenting skills and setting home conditions to support children as students
- Communicating: conducting effective communications from school-to-home

Currently in its sixth year, the program continues to seek ways to connect with its target population. When the Center was being discussed, surveys were developed to assess what needs might exist among the targeted immigrant families. The primary language groups have been and continue to be English, Polish, Spanish, and Gujarati. English-language surveys were translated into Polish, Spanish, and Gujarati and mailed to all households. The results from those surveys indicated that our English Language Learner (ELL) families were interested in English as a Second Language (ESL) classes, computer classes, and information about how American high schools operate. In response to the survey results, the Family Center program was designed to offer the types of experiences families indicated that they needed.

Eighth Grade Open House Initiative

For the past six years, breakout groups have been offered for the parents of incoming freshmen during the eighth grade open house. Led by staff who are fluent in the three "primary" languages, information is provided primarily about who the necessary people are in the school such as counselors, the ESL Department Chair, and the ESL faculty. Information is also given about the ESL program—how the levels are organized and which teachers teach which levels. Finally, information is also given about ESL classes for parents in the community.

ESL Classes

Beginning ESL classes had been offered through the Family Center for the first five years of the program. The classes were taught by an ESL faculty member and offered twice a week over a ten week period. Initially the classes were well attended, but attendance subsequently declined steadily. The local community college has begun to offer multiple levels of ESL classes within the high school building and enrollment in these continues to rise. It is probable that those who would have been taking a single ESL level-one class through the Family Center have moved on the take an ESL program through the community college. This has been seen as a welcomed outcome as parents and community members continue to take a variety of ESL classes in the high school rather than moving to the community college campus.

Computer Classes

Many parents indicated that they had few computer skills and wanted to learn more. Consequently, a basic computer class was developed that taught very basic computer skills—turning on the computer, creating a password, logging on and off, as well as logging on to the Internet, searching, and sending basic e-mail. The course is taught by an English-speaking member of the Applied Arts and Technology Department. As she is presenting the material in English, it is then interpreted in Polish, Gujarati, and Spanish by three members of the ESL department. This has been a well attended class that ends with a celebratory pizza party during which certificates of completion are presented.

As the Family Center program became established, it evolved, particularly recently. Originally the Family Center was focused on the immigrant population and it succeeded in establishing a strong connection with this group of parents. This was driven in part by the initial grants that limited the Family Center to addressing the needs of ELL families. As that grant money became less available, the scope of the Family Center was allowed to expand to address the possible needs of the parent population as a whole. While many of the families speak a language other than English at home, many are actually bilingual and would not have been targeted by the original grants and subsequent programs.

Expansion of the Family Center

In order to move forward with an expanded curriculum, parents were again surveyed about their current needs and a "Sounding Board" was created to tap into the wisdom of local agencies, service groups, and staff that would be able to evaluate suggested programs and provide needed direction. After seeking input from parents and the Sounding Board concerning ways in which the Family Center program could expand, collaborative relationships were established with the nearby community college, as well as with the nearby large hospital.

Parent Education Series

Three series have been developed for parents. *Welcome to Maine East* is scheduled for the spring semester following the February Eighth Grade Open House. The four-night series invites parents of the eighth graders who will soon be freshmen to learn more about the ways in which they might be involved at the high school through Fine Arts, Sports, Clubs and Organizations, and Student Government *Understanding the Freshman Experience* consists of four presentations by the social workers, the deans, the counselors, and the principal. It is offered during the fall semester. Each presentation focuses on relevant information and answers questions that the parents may have now that their son/daughter is attending the high school. *Parents as Partners* reaches out to parents who are concerned about adolescent drug and alcohol use. This is a task force of individuals and parents who are currently organizing a "Parents Who Host, Lose the Most" campaign targeting parents of high school students. The task force is also reaching out to the parents of fourth and fifth graders to help them navigate the middle school years drug-free. Furthermore, the task force cosponsors parent education events with a local youth service agency. Recently sponsored events included Parenting with Love and Logic and Teen Dating Violence.

Family Medicine Clinic

The high school currently has an in-house School-Based Health Center that is staffed and operated by Lutheran General Hospital. The staff includes a medical director, an adolescent medicine physician, a nurse practitioner, a mental health worker, and a secretary. The clinic is open during school hours year round and sees students—many of whom are either underinsured or do not have insurance at all.

Dr. Frank Belmonte, clinical director of the School-Based Health Center is a strong supporter of the need for the Friday Night Family Medicine Clinics. He believes that many of our students' parents and family members are underserved by the medical community. Of the 2196 students who are registered to seek clinic services, 511 were insured through the state's children's health insurance program, 630 had no health insurance, and 1055 had private insurance. As a result, discussions were held between the Lutheran General Hospital staff and the Family Center to create a once-a-month Family Medical Clinic. The clinic is open to residents of Maine Township. Patients are seen by Family Practice and Pediatric attending and resident physicians without charge. Patients are given a physical that includes diabetes and blood pressure screenings. During the two hours that this clinic is open, an average of 10–25 patients are seen, many who have not seen a physician in years.

Community College Workshops/Classes

Our local community college is sensitive to the needs of our diverse population. Currently they support a satellite site at the school and offer a variety of ESL classes as well as GED and standard Adult Education classes. Following a series of discussions with the college staff, the Family Center offers eight workshops and one class in partnership with the college. Preparation for Citizenship is a ten week, two-night per week preparation class for taking the citizenship exam. It is an intensive preparation course that enables participants to be fully able to pass the citizenship examination.

Furthermore, discussions are held about the application process, forms, and protocols.

Each of the workshops is one and a half to two hours long. Workshops are usually offered on those nights of the week when the community college classes are not being offered so attendance for those classes is not affected. The workshops use both didactic and discussion formats. Parents leave the workshop with handouts, and contact information for the workshop presenters. Four workshops focus on the transition to college highlighting the knowledge and skills needed to apply to college; the resources available for paying for college; understanding and completing financial aid forms; and navigating the transition involved with parenting a new college student. The remaining four workshops focus on work-related interests of parents. The topics include Understanding the American Job Market; Employee Rights and Responsibilities; The Citizenship Application Process; and Reviewing Foreign Educational Credentials.

Additional Opportunities through the Family Center

In addition to the clinic, classes, and workshops developed in collaboration with external partners, the Family Center continues to develop opportunities with in-house staff and resources. Coffee Cake and Conversation is held once a month. Members of the community college ESL classes are invited to arrive one hour before class for coffee, cake, and conversation. Volunteers from the community—many of whom are retired teachers—are paired with the ESL adult students for the hour during which they share a conversation so that the student has the opportunity to practice speaking English.

EVALUATION

Student Outcomes

The outcome data for the Advisory has taken the form of descriptive statistics. As can be seen in Table 5.2, comparison of the first five years indicates an overall 56% drop in the number of failures among the freshmen. We attributed the up-tick in failures are the end of the 2006–07 school year to the introduction of a new computer system which did not allow for the four week review of grades resulting in 12 weeks without feedback data. We believe that dearth of information resulted in a lack of attention by freshmen and the staff to academic problems. This was unfortunate. As can be seen, the prior semester was the best ever in school history with 84% of the students in advisories passing.

In addition to monitoring grades every four weeks, freshmen are surveyed during November to assess the ways in which they understand the

TABLE 5.2 Percent of Freshmen with One or More Failures 1999–2008

	Planning Years			Operating Years					
Semester	99/00	00/01	01/01	02/03	03/04	04/05	05/06	06/07	07/08
1st	28	30	29	37	25	23	28	16	19
2nd	26	25	24	27	22	18	23	23	21

purpose of Advisory and the degree to which they have become involved in school cocurricular activities. Ninety-six percent of the 304 freshman who surveyed during the 2007–08 school year indicated that they understood the overall goal of the program, typically answering "It helps us get through ninth grade," or "Helps with homework and getting used to High School." One student specifically stated that "the purpose of Freshman Advisory is to watch over us so we don't do anything stupid." Eighty-six percent indicated that they had participated in a cocurricular activity (joined a sports or fine arts group); 8% indicated that they had tried out for something but were cut and the remaining 4% of students hadn't been involved. Freshmen were also asked for their recommendations for improvement of the Advisory. Seventy-four percent indicated that they would keep it the same, or make it longer; 19% indicated they would want more time for studying and fewer activities; 4% wanted more free time in advisory; and the remaining 3% suggested that advisory should just meet during the first but not the second semester.

Family Center Outcomes

Attendance has been consistent at the clinic, computer classes, citizenship workshops, and parent education workshops. Positive feedback has been received about the medical clinic. Over the past year and a half, clinic physicians have treated a wide variety of concerns including chest pain, diabetic foot ulcers, rashes, infections, high blood sugar and blood pressure. One patient, with no insurance, hadn't seen a physician in over 25 years. Another patient was insured, but had a deductible of $5000.00 and a glucose level of 370. Patients are referred to other clinics for follow-up care. The clinic also completes routine school physicals. One mother stated "I am so glad I could get in here. I won't have insurance for another month, we just moved here for a new job and I really don't want my kids to stay at home for four weeks before they could start school [where a new physical is required for enrollment]."

The computer classes originally attracted 18–20 participants whose exit surveys indicated they had learned a great deal and had enjoyed the class.

One woman, whose comment reflected many that were received, stated "I never knew how to turn on computer—now I am sending e-mail to my family in Poland—that makes me happy—good!"

The first citizenship class was attended by nine adults who have continued to meet in a second spring class. Again, exit surveys have indicated that the participants are learning and enjoy the class. One of the students recently stated, "Here I am learning what I need to know for citizenship text. I am more sure of myself." Of the first nine, all planned to take the citizenship test within several months of completing the class.

There are 15 regulars at the Coffee, Cake, and Conversation group. "My English is very not good. It is difficult to speak, so it is good we talk together…is that right way to say that?" was a comment made by one of the regular group attendees. Conversational topics this year have ranged from telling one's immigration story to a recent discussion about election processes in Poland, Pakistan, South Africa, and the U.S.

Finally, the Love and Logic and Teen Dating Violence presentations collaboratively held with a community agency were well attended, attracting over 100 parents to each. Exit surveys indicated the following: 97% felt they learned some or a great deal about the topic; 100% indicated that the format and presenters were helpful, and over 75% wanted further information and or a class to further their understanding.

Continuing Challenges

Freshman Advisory Challenges

The Advisory is a work in progress and as such is challenged by the human components of the program. Each year, a new set of freshmen come to school, each year new advisory mentors and new Advisory teachers join the program, and each year new staff members must learn to take advantage of the resources available to them in the Advisory. Each human element presents a unique set of challenges and opportunities including:

- Freshmen are a work in progress. Although they have managed to complete junior high, many are not prepared to "do" high school until they have been in high school for the first year.
- Mentors have a hard time understanding the value of discussion and with processing the initiatives. They tend to clump in the front of the room. They have to role-play the initiatives so they can lead them in advisory.
- Supervising staff requires finding a balance between supporting the mentors as the primary deliverers of the curriculum and maintaining an environment that is conducive to the attainment of the Advi-

sory goals. Some are overly involved while others are underinvolved. Each acts as an independent contractor who shapes the individual advisory within the broad parameters of the planned program.

- Staff/Faculty perceiving the Freshman Advisory as part of the academic program. It is difficult to maintain a level of dialogue between Advisory staff and the freshman course teachers that supports the work the teachers are doing in the classroom.

Family Center Challenges

One of the most challenging issues of working within a highly diverse community is actually getting the parents into school to partake of the multiple programs that are available to them. Furthermore, our high school draws its student body from seven very unique communities with housing ranging from Section Eight apartments to multimillion dollar mega-mansions. Some of our programs have been very well attended and others have been underattended. In order to reach out to the existing community, the Family Center coordinator is a member of a variety of community coalitions that then in turn connect with the various constituencies in the community. Coalitions include three Healthy Communities Partnerships; a Human Needs Task Force, an Area Planning Committee; two Ministerial Committees, Advisory Boards of the School-Based Health Center, a nationally recognized after-school program of our elementary sender school district, a Hispanic Advisory Council, and a township-wide ant-idrug coalition.

Information about all the programs is made available in the four primary languages (English, Spanish, Polish, and Gujarati) and is sent to all families through a district mailing The materials are shared at each of the partner coalitions meetings and is sent (in English) as a part of the monthly Principal's newsletter. Finally, information is also posted on the school website and sent via e-mail to families in the sending elementary school district's Constant Connection system.

CONCLUSIONS

> One of the most difficult tasks we face as human beings is communicating meaning across individual differences, a task confounded immeasurably when we attempt to communicate across social lines, racial lines, cultural lines or lines of unequal power"(Delpit, 1995, p. 66).

"Developmental understanding" might be added to this list particularly as we begin to examine the ways in which students and their families navigate transitions in early adolescence from elementary to middle and middle to high school.

The transition to high school is complex. It is confounded by two intersecting issues. First, Eccles and her colleagues have strongly suggested younger adolescents typically do not have the developmental capacity to successfully transition between middle and high school on their own. Second, parents often perceive that the transition into high school is an opportune time to disengage from their children. Parents disengage for several reasons. Some do so based on an assumption that the child will be independent soon and it is important to "cut the apron strings". Others disengage believing that they may not have the experience, knowledge or time to be academically helpful to their son or daughter (Eccles & Harold, 1996). Comer (1996) suggests that a cultural dissonance between the parents and the school is at the heart of what diminishes parental involvement.

This chapter has presented information about the ways in which one large and highly diverse high school has sought to support students and their families during the transition to high school. The work is grounded in prevailing research about adolescence and about parents all the while being situated the day to day idiosyncrasies of applied practice. As challenging as this might be at this critical transition, when students may be developmentally ill-equipped, parents may be disengaging, it becomes incumbent upon schools to support students and engage parents.

REFERENCES

Booth, A. & Dunn, J. F. (1996). *Family–school links: How do they affect educational outcomes?* Mahwah, NJ: Erlbaum.

Bronfenbrenner, U. & Morris, P. A. (1998). The ecology of developmental processes. *The Handbook of Child Psychology, 1,* 993–1028

Delpit, L. (1995). *Other people's children: Cultural conflict in the classroom.* New York: New Press, NY.

Eccles, J. S. (2004). Schools, academic motivation and stage–environment fit. In Lerner & Steinberg (2nd ed.), *Handbook of adolescent psychology.* Hoboken, NJ: John Wiley & Sons.

Eccles, J. S.,& Harold, R.D. (1996), Family involvement in children's and adolescents' schooling. In A. Booth & J. Dunn (Eds.) *Family–School links: How do they affect educational outcomes?* (pp. 3–34). Mahwah NJ: Erlbaum.

Epstein, J. L., et al. (2002). *School, family, and community partnerships: Your handbook for action* (2nd ed.). Thousand Oaks, CA: Corwin Press.I

Feinstein, S. (2004). *Secrets of the teenage brain.* Thousand Oaks, CA: Corwin Press.

Fischer, K. (2006, November). Opening remarks HGSE Conference: Learning and the Brain, Boston.

Haynes, N. & Ben-Avie, M. (1996) Parents as full partners in education. In A. Booth & J. Dunn (Eds.) *Family–school links: How d othey affect educational outcomes?* (pp. 45–55). Mahwah NJ: Erlbaum.

Joyner, E., Comer, J., & Ben-Avie, M. (2004). *Transforming school leadership and management to support students learning and development: The field guide to Comer schools* www.comerprocess.org.

Mizelle, N. (1999). *Helping middle school students make the transition to high school.* ERIC Digest, National Parent Information Network.

Mizelle, N. & Irvin, J. (2005, May). Transition from middle school into high school. *Middle School Journal, 31*, No. 5.

Yale Child Study Center (2004). *Six pathways to healthy child development and academic success.* Thousand Oaks, CA: Corwin Press.

CHAPTER 6

THE FOXFIRE APPROACH TO STUDENT AND COMMUNITY INTERACTION

Hilton Smith

Though students reside in their own communities, and some may even have a sense of attachment to that community, most will make their way through and out of their respective communities with little grasp of what can be learned there or what they could contribute. In the process of growing up in a community, students absorb their communities' prevailing attitudes and habits of mind in an unreflective and uncritical process that tends to impair the development of the skills and dispositions essential for effective citizenship. Evidence of that impairment abounds in the poor performance of U.S. citizens on national and international tests of history and geography, including the kind of provincial ignorance of cultures and geopolitics that enables U.S. political leaders to embark on ill-advised ventures abroad.

Teachers in the U.S. at all grade levels use their communities as resources for instruction for many subjects, from third-grade trips to the local fire station, to interviews of Viet Nam veterans by eleventh grade history students, to inviting bankers to talk to economics classes about credit cards. While pedagogically worthwhile, those practices involve one-way relationships

Promising Practices for Family and Community Involvement during High School, pages 89–103

with communities, rather than the reciprocity entailed in "connecting" with communities. Foxfire's Core Practice #6 emphasizes that reciprocity:

> Connections between the classroom work, the surrounding communities, and the world beyond the communities are clear. Course content is connected to the community in which the learners live. Learners' work will "bring home" larger issues by identifying attitudes about and illustrations of those issues in their home community. (Paris et al., 2005)

The results, when the connection is made, include (a) ongoing engagement with the content of the subject, requiring a minimal use of "classroom control" measures; (b) durable learning—acquiring skills, knowledge and attitudes that persist after assessments and grades; and (c) an appreciation of the academic field and an appetite to learn more. Those are the criteria we used in developing Foxfire's Core Practices (which can be seen at http://www.foxfire.org/teaching.html).

Following a few examples of Foxfire practitioners' students working with their communities, is a summary of the evolution of what came to be referred to as "the Foxfire approach," followed by more examples illustrating student work with communities. Assembling a sample of Foxfire practitioners' narratives as examples of communities as educational texts provided an opportunity to view Foxfire in the context of some of the recent literature dealing with that pedagogical dimension. The closing consists of some advocacies about practices, as well as some cautions, or warning labels.

Examples of connections that ground readers in the community text provide examples that frame the subsequent description of the approach. The first example is drawn from my own classroom practice:

> In a twelfth-grade government and economics class using *TIME* magazine as the initial source of topics, one group of students learned about the compact between the states in the southeast to rotate storage of nuclear wastes to each state in a preset order. Then they learned that one of the sites being considered next was in the mountainous county just across the state line from where they lived. They dug into the literature about nuclear wastes, and then began attending the hearings being held in that county. They taped interviews with people attending the hearings, both residents and government agency representatives. Because they had learned about nuclear wastes, they could ask informed questions that could not be dismissed as "kid" questions. Their presence and questions actually affected the outcome of the hearings, which were cancelled after only about half had been completed. During all this they reported back to the class (and other classes), so that we all benefitted from what they learned. We learned about politics and government and economics never found in a textbook or a teacher's lecture. (Smith, 1999)

The second example provides a sweeping picture of the possibilities of putting schools in the center of their communities. Jerry Hoffman describes the initiatives of the School at the Center program in Nebraska:

> Young citizens in Albion, Arthur, Big Springs, Cook, Crete, Henderson, Morrill, Talmage, Wakefield, Wallace... are documenting their local heritage by recording the stories of elders, making music from the stories, painting public murals, and preserving local historic architecture. They are also learning about new immigrants from Asia, Central and South America, and eastern Europe, and discovering common political and economic purposes for relocation. They are creating small businesses to meet the needs of the community and to engage in trade with other communities. They are learning about their environmental surroundings and working to preserve the soil, water, and air for the clean production of food and water. They are building new homes and renovating older homes for young families, elderly persons, and couples. And they are using the Internet to access information that is useful for local community and economic development self-study. (Hoffman, 1999)

The third example illustrates the value of attending to immediate situations that touch students' concerns that might never come to the surface with conventional modes of instruction. A sixth grade language arts class in Hall County, Georgia, decided to create child safety flyers for other students and their parents, stimulated by the abduction and murder of a girl their age a few days earlier. The flyers were distributed widely throughout the county and were acknowledged as being more effective than the adult-created material usually provided. (Briscoe, 1988)

The next example has the potential of inspiring all sorts of cross-grade curricular adaptations. At Puyallup High School, Tacoma, Washington, Carol Coe, a Foxfire-oriented teacher, was challenged by the very skeptical chemistry teacher to make the case to his students that they could acquire an academically sound knowledge of chemistry using the Foxfire approach. During Carol's discussion with the class, the students agreed that the best way to learn a subject is to teach it. A curriculum match was found between the subjects in the chemistry course and the prescribed science content at a nearby elementary school. The chemistry class students prepared lessons for the elementary students, discovering in the process how difficult it can be to translate material you thought you knew into material accessible to younger learners. In the process, they mastered the chemistry, as attested to by their test scores.

In each of those examples, the reciprocity is evident in the relationship between community and classroom. Also evident is the fact that the students acquired important knowledge of the subjects being studied. That needs to be stated because the notion of "projects" sometimes conjures teacher-designed, keep-busy, "fun" activities that do not necessarily entail durable learning. One of John Dewey's motivations for writing *Experience and Education* was the growing concern among some educators about exactly that kind of class activit. (Dewey, 1938). Dewey knew that our propensity for "either/or thinking" could lead to a rejection by those educators of the kind of student-centered experience he advocated and was practiced by many progressive educators. As will be evident from what follows, the individuals involved in the development of Foxfire took Dewey's counsel very seriously.

THE FOXFIRE APPROACH

Evolution of Foxfire

In 2007, Foxfire celebrated forty years of continuous publication of *The Foxfire Magazine* by students at Rabun County High School by publishing the thirteenth in the series of Foxfire books, *The Foxfire 40th Anniversary Book* (Cheek et al., 2006), which was also created by those students as a summer project. During those forty years, Foxfire evolved from a high school cultural journalism project into what we came to refer to as the "Foxfire approach," a set of pedagogical practices teachers can adapt for any grade level, subject area, and student group (Wigginton, 1991, especially "The Circle Grows"). The key term is "adapt." The Foxfire approach is not a neat template to be acquired in a one-day professional development session, then implemented in class next week. Our approach to dissemination is to provide intensive, critical immersion in workshops that model the approach, usually in summer sessions, after which each practitioner figures out how to make the adaptations to her/his students, class by class, year by year. By using the term "approach," we intend to convey the vision that the Foxfire Core Practices become habits of mind, rather than an activity in a repertoire of practices to be employed occasionally—"today let's use Foxfire to study..."

Foxfire's Core Practices provide stimulus and guidance to teachers who made those adaptations. However, unlike scripted, sequential instructional "methods" that a teacher can check off as they are completed, the Core Practices elude our best efforts to fulfill all of them all in any given class at any given time, similar to the way Jefferson envisioned our pursuit of the fulfillment of the ideals of democracy. The title of Foxfire founder Eliot Wigginton's book, *Sometimes a Shining Moment*, aptly conveys the spirit of the Foxfire enterprise for teachers (Wigginton, 1986). Those "moments," however rare and ephemeral, make the pursuit worthwhile, especially knowing that the students experience the same affective lift.

From Foxfire's beginning, the community served as the audience and affirmation for the work of creating a magazine focused on the rich lore of this Appalachian region. Many of our students held a diminished view of themselves and their culture, reinforced by media stereotypes of mountain people, such as the movie *Deliverance* (which was filmed in the immediate area). Discovering— and sharing—the enterprise and resilience of mountain people generated an enhanced sense of self-esteem, as well as the drive to acquire the varied skills to produce quality articles.

Foxfire's evolution into a full-range approach began in 1987 with a grant of $1.5 million from the Bingham Trust of Connecticut to disseminate Foxfire practices broadly, well beyond our experience in assisting English and journalism teachers to establish their own version of the Foxfire magazine project.

Three Professional Development Principles

At the outset we established three givens to be followed. First, teachers involved in any sort of professional development about Foxfire had to elect to do so by making informed decisions. As classroom teachers with considerable unsatisfactory experiences with "in-service" programs forced onto us by well-intentioned administrators, we recognized that lending our energies to that kind of dissemination would be the kiss of death.

Second, we also knew that the history of efforts to improve schooling was littered with the derelicts of promising innovations that never attained enough traction to endure. In the year following the summer's inspirational workshop, it is very hard to sustain that vision and effort in the face of the prevailing, subtly coercive patterns of schooling. So we elected to take Foxfire to regional groups of teachers who agreed up front to form networks of like-minded peers to help each other figure out how to adapt Foxfire's Core Practices to their own unique circumstances. The result was the formation of Foxfire teacher networks. All the examples of using the community as educational texts that follow come from teachers in those networks.

Third, the facilitators of our workshops had to model the Foxfire approach—walk the talk—so the participants would both see the approach in action and get a sense of what their own students might experience. That included participating in making decisions about how to fulfill the "givens" of the workshops, small group work, and considering audiences for their work. Modeling the approach meant digging into the philosophical underpinnings of the approach, something we anticipated that teachers would be very reluctant to do: "Don't bother me with the theory! If it works, just tell me how to do it!" Even so, a thorough and critical examination of John Dewey's *Experience and Education* (Dewey, 1938) became standard practice in our workshops for teachers. That experience provides both a philosophical framework for considering the Foxfire approach and an increased awareness of the possibilities for creating learning experiences that engage students and result in durable learning (Gibbs and Howley, 2000).

What happened in the following years affirmed the efficacy of those three features of our Teacher Outreach Program, as well as our trust that teachers have the skills, perseverance and caring nature to adapt the Core Practices to their own situations. As they did so, collaborating within and beyond their regional networks, those teachers owned "the approach." Foxfire became the province of its practitioners, not a product of a prepackaged program.

Because Foxfire developed as a local initiative, without conscious reference to any movement or trend or philosophical orientation, our discovery of how Foxfire fit into the larger scheme of education came as revelations. In the early years, Wigginton was encouraged to consider the pedagogical ideas of John Dewey for the next level of development of Foxfire (Wigginton, 1991). That led to the clarification of the possibilities of Foxfire beyond a student-generated magazine about local culture, as well as a challenge to contribute to a tradition of schooling that had real potential for improving the experiences of students in substantive ways. That tradition of schooling, a strand in the progressive education movement exemplified in the work of John Dewey, became evident to us shortly after Foxfire began to gain national attention. We received a congratulatory, affirming letter and clippings from a retired educator in Ohio, describing the cultural journalism projects he and his students generated in the 1930s!

Core Practices

As Foxfire evolved, so did the Core Practices, as new practitioners' insights stimulated additions and refinements to the Practices. (At present we are beginning to consider another set of refinements.) Specific Core Practices are illuminated in the examples provided in the next section. As perspective for what follows, however, the eleven current Core Practices (http://www.foxfire.org/teaching.html) could be woven together this way:

> The orientation of the Foxfire Approach is contained in the first lines of Core Practice #1: "The work teachers and learners do together is infused from the beginning with learner choice, design, and revision." That work is to be characterized by "academic integrity" (#3) and "connected to the community" (#6). The "role of the teacher is that of facilitator and collaborator" (#2), who makes sure "the work is characterized by active learning" (#4) that engages students' "imagination and creativity" (#9) and makes effective use of "peer teaching, small group work, and teamwork" (#5). The work provides the most durable learning when it addresses "an audience beyond the teacher" (#7), and includes "rigorous, ongoing assessment and evaluation" (#10). "Reflection is an essential activity" (#11) during the processes of working together

and as a synthesis of what has been learned. Finally, when the approach is fully engaged "new activities spiral gracefully out of the old" (#8).

Note the frequent use of "work" in the Core Practices. No other term seems apt for describing what students and their teachers do when using the Foxfire Approach. While the prevailing stereotype of high school students characterizes them as work-aversive, our experience is that they really feel energized and fulfilled when their efforts pay off in understanding the world around them, while affirming them as individuals and achieving something substantive in their communities. Note also that "fun" never appears in the examples which follow.

Foxfire Endeavors with Strong Community Connections

The narratives provided below represent different regions, demographic situations, and content areas. Each presents a different way that educators have grounded learning in the community enabling students to learn and develop through participation in their community.

Constructing Community Space

Elk City, Idaho, is at the end of civilization. The last bit of paved road leads to the K–12 school. Past the genuine boardwalk town center, the roads turn to dirt and fade as they enter the awesome natural beauty of the Snake Wilderness Area. That beauty, however, could not hide the fact that Elk City was experiencing declining fortunes. The lumber mill had downsized to one shift. Two Forest Service Wilderness Ranger Districts had been combined, with many of the rangers transferred out of the area. "The population was dropping and opinions on why it was happening and what to do about it seemed split between the mill, the Forest Service, the environmentalists, and others," recalls Suzie Borowicz, a Foxfire-trained teacher who served as the K–12 school's principal. She adds, "A sense of mistrust was growing and something needed to be done about it."

A member of the community, Ian Barlow, thought that a community project might bring various factions together. The school is the center of this community, he noted, and the school needed a place for performing arts. Mrs. Borowicz liked the idea. A steering committee composed of students, teachers, school staff, and community members developed plans for two classrooms (Core Practice #9): One for art activities and another for science classroom/lab/greenhouse with room for community meetings. Later, a performing arts building and a large outdoor classroom gazebo were added to the plans (Core Practice #7).

The students took on major roles: surveying the site and calculating the amount of dirt to be removed; writing grant proposals; contacting the National Timber Framers Guild for their assistance in the construction (Core Practices #4, #5, and #9). Students were actively engaged alongside adults in the community in the actual construction (Core Practice #6).

The Gazebo went up first. Suzie Borowicz describes the scene:

> After we got it up, we held a dinner at the school. There was live music and it was a wonderful time. I walked out to the Gazebo. The roof sheathing wasn't up yet, just the timbers. The moon was out and it was a wonderful experience and I had great hopes for our town. If we could pull together like this to build the Gazebo, we could and would get the performing arts center built.

And they did (Hatton, 2000). This project is an excellent example of the "power of place" illuminated by Sharon Bishop in her work with the Annenberg Rural Challenge (Bishop, 2004).

Being Historians

The next example provides a dramatic contrast in settings—from the deep forests of Idaho to the center of a major city in the southeastern U.S. The intersection of two developments in Atlanta, Georgia, provided an opportunity for the ninth grade humanities class at Booker T. Washington High School (BTWHS) to apply their curriculum in an active and productive way. The humanities program received a grant to develop an oral history project on "Old Atlanta." At about the same time, the leaders of Atlanta announced plans to build a domed stadium. That entailed the razing of Vine City, one of the oldest African-American neighborhoods in the center of Atlanta. The humanities class instructors realized that would be an ideal focus for the humanities class oral history project. The resulting project, developed by the students (Core Practice #1), was to interview the residents in Vine City to create an oral history of that historic area before the community members were dispersed by the domed stadium construction.

Though only a few BTWHS students lived in Vine City, all of them knew about it. The class developed an interview protocol, then proceeded to interview the residents (Core Practice #4). They taped the interviews, then transcribed them. They also photographed the area extensively, so there would be a visual accompaniment for the collected interviews.

During this process, Foxfire sent a crew from the Foxfire Magazine class to BTWHS, then hosted a visit by students and teachers from BTWHS to Rabun County High School to learn the process of developing the interview transcriptions into accessible narratives that retained the voice of the Vine City inhabitants (Core Practices #2 and #5).

BTWHS teacher Katie Lindquist's reflections convey the spirit and value of the project:

Frequently, interviews are with city leaders. However, our interviews represent a cross-section of the community, including retired, life-long residents, as well as young shop owners. It is our hope that others will learn from this effort and will enjoy this work as much as our students have. Because of his interview work, one student has developed a serious interest in community politics and is thinking of a political career.

Two students were invited by Eliot Wigginton to talk about the domed stadium project at an Apple Corps breakfast in Atlanta. This exposure was beneficial to those students in developing their self-confidence in making a presentation before an audience. Now they are anxious to talk with other groups about this project. Likewise, we gained volunteer help through Apple Corps in transcribing some of our tapes." (Lindquist, 1988)

Another aspect of this project deserves mention. The domed stadium project stirred up old racial conflicts in Atlanta, "the city too busy to hate." From the perspective of the Vine City residents and some social activists, the stadium project seemed to run roughshod over the residents of this genuinely historic neighborhood. Advocates for the stadium project, of course, promoted it as an economic boon for a city that was growing into major league status. They saw the resistance as nearsighted and simply obstructionist. No one could claim that the BTWHS students' work resolved that conflict, but the Vine City residents could at least know that some of the rich heritage of their neighborhood had been preserved.

Teachers reading this deserve to know that the BTWHS students' dispositions toward the Vine City project were not immediately positive. Like most young people in the U.S., they did not appreciate the value of people like the residents of Vine City. The BTWHS teachers' skill in involving the students right away in defining the project (Core Practice #1) and providing an authentic product (Core Practice #7), led that class to the connection to the community (Core Practice #6). By the students' own accounts, they developed ownership of the project gradually. Sometimes that is the best way. The finished project resides in the permanent collection of the Atlanta Historical Society (Core Practice #6).

Appreciating Cultural Heritage

The publication of *The Foxfire Book* (Wigginton 1972) generated interest in English and journalism teachers around the U.S. and abroad, including those in schools primarily for minorities. One of the earliest efforts to share the magazine experience, for example, was a trip to a Native American reservation in New Mexico. The following example, also involving Native Americans, demonstrates the power of the Foxfire approach when it is shared by teachers in several disciplines, including visual art.

In the center of the gym at Lapwai High School in Lapwai, Idaho, on a spring evening in April, 1990, a series of interlocking 4'x 8' display panels ran the full length of the basketball court. Student artwork covered both sides of all the panels (Core Practice #10). Nearly all the artwork drew on Native American themes, primarily Lapwai (Core Practice #9). Down one side of the bleachers and across one end of the gym, the families of the students displayed traditional crafts, such as bead and leather work (Smith, 1990).

This community display was extraordinary because it represented the coming together of three generations of Native Americans (Core Practice #6), the result of the combined efforts of a small group of Foxfire teachers, especially the art teacher, Linda Boyer, who had gently guided her charges into an appreciation of the themes and skills of their heritage. Prior to that, the community had been riven by the kind of conflict unfortunately typical of some Native American areas. The students tended to reject their cultural heritage, especially the male students, who preferred motorcycles, beer, and drugs. The elders, of course, did not understand their adolescents' attitudes. The exhibit on that April evening did not heal all the sores of that conflict, of course. It did, however, provide a way toward a peace treaty (Boyer, 1990).

Benefits of the Foxfire Approach

Two elements in these examples warrant comment. The Foxfire Approach embraces the view that the disciplines of the arts and sciences are elegant, useful epistemologies—windows onto the world, nature, and human behavior. Unfortunately, experiences in school tend to convey a sense that the disciplines are static repositories of multiple-choice, short-answer information. When the Core Practices guide instruction, students experience those disciplines as dynamic, evolving discourses. Students involved in the projects described above related their experiences to the disciplines, using the modes of inquiry of the disciplines, thereby acquiring a sense of the power of these disciplines to try to make sense of experiences.

However, it is the other element that sets students' experiences for durable learning as well as an appetite to learn more: the affective dimension. Emotions associated with effort and fulfillment—often beyond the ability to be expressed in words—tie content to experience to community. So much schooling seems to drain away emotional content, as if it might be dangerous or inappropriate. The students involved in the projects described above were excited—and their excitement served to sustain their efforts and to set what they learned as a permanent habit of mind.

Foxfire's reputation as a successful instructional strategy that engages students with their communities rests on solid achievements (Gibbs and Howley, 2000). The *Foxfire Magazine* has been continuously published for forty-two years by students at Rabun County High School. There are about 4000 Foxfire-influenced P–16 classroom practitioners around the U.S. The wealth of narratives by those practitioners attests to the dynamic, adaptable nature of the Foxfire enterprise. Describing that enterprise with validating references to quantitative research and theory would be misleading, since Foxfire developed and evolved as pragmatic responses to the challenges and opportunities present at any school, not as a conscious effort to implement in practice a theoretical structure, nor contribute consciously to research about teaching and learning.

CONCLUSIONS

Warning Labels

Readers may note that most of the examples provided to illustrate connections with communities occurred before the current burdens of accountability and standards made explorations beyond the classroom difficult to justify and arrange. In reality, Foxfire practitioners always and everywhere had to swim against the prevailing patterns of conventional schooling, not to avoid prescribed curricula, but to go beyond the minimums defined by those curricula. In today's contexts, the Foxfire approach serves as an antidote to the boring drudgery of teacher-centered, textbook-focused, test-driven instruction. Foxfire teachers acknowledge up front the givens of prescribed curricula, including preparation for standardized tests, then work with their students to build on those givens to engage in work that can transcend the limits of one-size-fits-all teaching.

Recent participants in Foxfire courses for teachers provided by the newly formed Foxfire–Piedmont Partnership teach in school districts deeply committed to improving scores on standardized tests. They are learning how to deal with that agenda while employing the Foxfire approach. We expect to have some examples of those successes with a year or two.

Sometimes advocates of particular notions about teaching neglect to include warning labels. Herewith are three that go with the Foxfire approach.

First, educators considering the Foxfire approach are hereby forewarned that instituting it is hard work, especially in the early engagements with students who have become accustomed to teacher-centered, text-focused, test-driven classroom instruction (Martin, 2001). High school students who have learned how to succeed in those contexts can be very resistant to anything new. Students for whom schooling has been an unrewarding experience are equally difficult to reach. Adding to the mix are teachers whose experience is limited to conventional modes of instruction and are thereby made reluctant to "experiment," especially if the outcome seems dubious.

Less secure teachers are also understandably hesitant to go to the edge. Then there are administrators who are adverse to anything that might create problematic situations for them to deal with.

Second, if you succeed, other teachers may resent that success, especially if (a) your students talk about it in front of other teachers, and (b) the work gets local media attention. Our counsel is to anticipate that by being modest and avoiding becoming an irritating advocate.

Third, some projects lead into hazardous waters. In a suburb of Chicago, for example, students' interest in a polluted lake in the local park led to an investigative project, clearly labeled as "science," by the way, that found the major polluter to be a large industry that was the largest employer in the region. Exciting, yes, but the resulting furor stressed all the adults involved, including the superintendent. The message here is not to back off, but to keep everyone even remotely touched by the work in the loop. A favorite Foxfire adage is "Never surprise the principal."

Closing Thoughts

Given all that, why would any teacher take the plunge to try the Foxfire approach? From our workshops for teachers we have gleaned some answers: (a) "What we've been doing isn't working. The kids aren't really learning, just passing." (b) "I'm bored and I know they are bored." (c) "I noticed how engaged Mrs. G's students are in her math classes. I want that kind of engagement." (d) "I sorta lost the idealism of my teacher training. I'd like to get that back."

One thing we have learned that we communicate to interested teachers, including college instructors, is that while the Foxfire approach may work *against* the grain of conventional instruction practices, it does work *with* the grain of how we learn—by constructing meaning from every experience. The experiences of every student include those in her/his community (Smith, 2002). Why not start there with classroom practices?

In regard to classroom practices, opportunities for connections to communities do not always arrive full-blown, like the razing of Vine City or community leaders in Elk City recognizing the possibilities for community bonding through constructing facilities for their school. In most situations it takes time for teachers to lead students to the possibilities for community connections, like that at Lapwai High School. Some Foxfire practitioners share the Core Practices with their classes, so at least the prospects of more authentic learning are available for students to consider.

Know that the teachers in each of the examples had moments of doubt and uncertainty. Sometimes students lose interest and ambitious plans slide off the rails, as happened to this teacher more than once. We are, after all, working with adolescents. Rather than bail out and revert to what is familiar and comfortable, however, those occasions can be some of the most potent in guiding students toward truly productive engagement. What did we learn? What did we do well? How could we improve *next time*?

Three instructional practices characterize the work of teachers who succeed in the hard work of implementing the Core Practices. First is to saturate instruction with clearly stated purposes, communicated to and developed with students. Take seriously the perennial student plaint, "Why do we have to know this?" The question deserves an answer, not "because I said so," or "because we have to." In fact, a worthy objective for all teaching is to eliminate the first-person singular pronoun from all instructional statements, such as "Now I want you to . . .".

Second, develop a repertoire of assessments that provide genuine feedback to you and the students about who is learning (and not learning). We commend the work of Grant Wiggins as an excellent resource for designing those kinds of assessments (Wiggins, 1998). In this regard, Foxfire practitioners stress the value of de-emphasizing grades, which tend to reward short-term learning, preferring instead to use assessments to guide instruction toward improving student performance.

Finally, debrief, debrief, debrief. Debriefings can provide honest feedback about how things are going, what is being learned, what is not yet understood, how procedures need to be altered, how things might be done differently, and whether the class is coming together as a community. Debriefings can also serve as transitions to new activities, as well as a kind of break. Students soon come to expect and appreciate debriefings—and can begin conducting the debriefings.

Assessments and debriefings provide opportunities for both students and teachers to articulate *what is being learned that is not necessarily being taught*, a very important (and neglected) aspect of student achievement.

In *A Time to Learn*, George Wood describes high schools as "democracy's finishing school" (Wood, 2005). The overarching vision of Foxfire is to provide experiences that result in students acquiring the skills and dispositions needed to function effectively as citizens in a democracy. Connecting with our communities holds the best promise for those kinds of experiences, a dimension for which Sharon Bishop makes an excellent case (Bishop, 2004).

In that vein, it seems appropriate to close with a vignette that provides an antidote to the kind of provincialism that can accompany the exploration of local communities as texts.

In June 1992, a group of students involved in a Foxfire-inspired cross-curricular program at Theodore Roosevelt High School in the Bronx made the trek from New York to the Foxfire Center in Rabun County, Georgia.

The trip involved three firsts for most of them: flying; being out of the city; and visiting a rural area.

While visiting the Foxfire gift shop, two students spotted *The Foxfire Book of Toys and Games* and began thumbing through the chapters on games (Page & Smith, 1993) Almost immediately they found games Appalachian kids played in yards and playgrounds that they also played, adapted for streets and sidewalks. That led to "Toys in the Hood," a diversionary project very different from their work on the core of their coursework, the juvenile justice system.

They never brought "Toys in the Hood" to completion—too many competing priorities—but we gleaned a lesson from that experience, reinforced many times since then: While exploring our respective communities as "educational texts" enables our students to discover much about themselves and their cultures, the equally powerful discovery is that apparently dissimilar cultures and communities share many practices, memes, and diversions. Could anything be more relevant and valuable today?

REFERENCES

Bishop, S. (2004), The power of place, *English Journal, 93*(6), 65–69.

Boyer, L. (1990). Learning that is Lasting, *Hands On,* 35–36, 91–94.

Briscoe, E. (1988). Child Safety—A booklet produced by a sixth grade class. *Hands On, 31,* 4–8.

Cheek, A., Nix, L. H., & Foxfire Students (Eds.)., (2006). *The Foxfire 40th Anniversary Book.* New York: Anchor Books.

Gibbs, T. and Howley, A. (2000). *"World-class standards" and local pedagogies: Can we do both?* Charleston, WV: ERIC Clearinghouse on Rural Education and Small Schools.(ERIC Document Reproduction Service No. EDO-RC-008)

Dewey, J. (1998). *Experience and Education: The60th Anniversary Edition.* West Lafayette, IN: Kappa Delta Pi.

Hatton, S. D. (2000), They Can Do It: Kids Take On Primary Role in Community Project, *Active Learner, 5* (1), 30–33.

Hoffman, J. (1999). Opinion—To those who lived before us and those yet to be born. *Active Learner, 4* (1). 22–24.

Lindquist, K. (1988, Summer). The Vine City domed stadium project, *Hands On, 32,* 17–19.

Martin, J. (2001). Learning to teach students in the community and environment. *Clearing Magazine, 110,* 10–13.

Page, L. G. & Smith, H. (1993). *The Foxfire book of Toys and Games.* Chapel Hill, NC: University of North Carolina Press.

Paris, C. (Ed.), (2005), *The Foxfire Course for Teachers.* Mountain City, GA: The Foxfire Fund.

Paris, C. (Ed.). *Foxfire Level One Course Book.* Mountain City, GA: Foxfire Fund Inc.

Smith, G. (1998). Rooting children in place. *Encounter, 11*(4), 13–24.

Smith, H. (1990), To Teachers and Their Students: The question is "How Can We learn?" Not "What Are We Going To Do Today?" In C. McDermott (Ed.), *Beyond the Silence* (pp. 24–32). Portsmouth NH: Heinemann.

Wiggins, G. (1998). *Educative Assessment: Designing Assessments to Inform and Improve Student Performance.* San Francisco: Jossey-Bass.

Wigginton E. (1972). *The Foxfire Book.* New York: Doubleday.

Wigginton, E. (1986). *Sometimes a Shining Moment.* Garden City NY: Anchor.

Wigginton, E. (1991). *Foxfire: Twenty-Five Years.* New York: Doubleday.

Wood, G. H. (2005). *Time to learn: How to create high schools that serve all students.* Portsmouth, NH: Heinemann.

CHAPTER 7

CAREER EDUCATION PARTNERSHIPS WITH BUSINESSES, POSTSECONDARY INSTITUTIONS, AND COMMUNITY ORGANIZATIONS THROUGH CONSEQUENTIAL LEARNING

Jack Shelton

Consequential Learning (CL) is the name that I have given to an educational approach developed primarily through my experience with PACERS (2007), an association of small public schools and communities in rural Alabama.

> CL is an educational approach advocating that all students be provided opportunities to use and master tools and concepts of the various academic,

Promising Practices for Family and Community Involvement during High School, pages 105–119

> business, and arts disciplines in order to produce significant public outcomes beneficial to themselves and their schools and communities and that invite local and professional evaluation and support (Shelton, 2005).

The approach has been implemented in more than forty schools through projects in a variety of areas including science, history, arts, and publishing. Projects have often been proposed by teachers who serve as sponsors and who are supported by professional consultants. Project outcomes require tools, information, and competence usually not found in schools. As a result the introduction of external organizations (such as postsecondary institutions, professional associations, publishers), professionals, information resources, and equipment is needed. Building upon students' capacity and willingness to undertake professional level and community beneficial work, the process connects them to professionals, postsecondary institutions, and career options. For example in one PACERS' program, rural students have, with the assistance of professionals and journalism students, published newspapers for their communities. This practice has resulted in strong collegial connections between students, teachers, and professional "outsiders." Students have gained marketable skills, entrepreneurial experience, personal confidence, and self-understanding as journalists and have created de facto portfolios and specific career interests. Therefore, although the approach is not per se about career education, its application results in the development of vocational skills, interests, and options for young people and serves as an example of how schools might begin preparing students for life beyond school by merging career development and academic learning as recommended by the National Commission on the High School Senior (2001).

PACERS

PACERS supports the development of multiple-site projects in order to extend resources, create a stronger research base, and establish a statewide cadre of teachers and students. To insure inclusivity PACERS projects are geographically, ethnically, and economically representative of rural Alabama. They have involved thousands of students and more than 250 teacher-sponsors. Projects are hosted by schools that generally have limited financial resources and high rates of students receiving free and reduced lunch. Supported by private foundations, public funds, and local schools and communities, the Consequential Learning approach has been implemented in more than forty schools through PACERS projects in a variety of areas including science, history, arts, and publishing. Participation in projects have led to higher scores in science and writing, increased student awareness of and appreciation for their communities, and strong teacher affirmation of the process and especially for its connection to their personal goals for teaching.

In this chapter principles of and results from Consequential Learning will be referenced in descriptions of two PACER Projects: PACERS' Community Newspaper Project (PCNP) and PACERS Rural Science for Life initiative. For these and all other projects, PACERS provides professional consultants, basic funding for equipment and supplies, and workshops and teaching materials for teachers. Teachers receive stipends for workshop participation and for developing lesson plans and other instructional resources. Issues that will be addressed include creating authentic learning contexts, identifying relevant projects, recruiting "outsiders," resources for teachers, academic outcomes and potential, and organizing local community support. Throughout the chapter career implications will be noted and collected into a summary at its conclusion.

Community Newspaper Project

Operating for two decades, the PCNP has involved a total of about forty small public schools in rural Alabama with thirteen schools currently participating. Elementary, middle, and high schools are included. Papers are produced in class and/or extracurricular settings. Staffs average about 15, however, papers often become a writing venue for an entire school. In the PCNP students publish *community* newspapers. Although they have a great deal of school-related content, given the central nature of schools in rural communities the papers are community papers. They operate as commercial papers with students expected to prepare business plans, sell ads, and cover the life of the community. This process engages students and local people and the school with the community. Students are supported by professionals including magazine editors, journalists, and journalism faculty and students from Auburn University and the University of Alabama.

Publishing a community paper is different from publishing a school paper. Students cover an entire community, and their publication reaches beyond the school to a public audience. Papers are expected to be self-sustaining as any business would; therefore, students must create and sell a worthy product, engage a variety of publics, manage money, and gather, analyze, and interpret information. These are challenging and locally significant tasks that have strong career relevance and that are essential for success. To complete these tasks, newspapers require an efficiently functioning staff which is a context for developing a very basic career skill—the capacity for working with others.

Rural Science for Life Initiative

Rural Science for Life: Sun, Soil, and Water is built upon three factors germane to the life of rural Alabama: plenty of sun, a great deal of freshwater, and land and traditions that can support agriculture. Beginning with the recognition of these resources, the Rural Science for Life program supports aquaculture, passive solar, and gardening/greenhouse initiatives.

CONSEQUENTIAL LEARNING PRINCIPLES

Authentic Learning Spaces

Effective contexts for learning are crucial for students' success and interest. *Where* students learn is an essential component of Consequential Learning, and the "where" is broadly defined to include classrooms, contexts that can be identified as "living labs," communities, and even the group of persons involved in a particular initiative. Although "where" may not be emphasized in schools, it is tacitly recognized as important by educators. For example the usually agreed upon value of field trips underscores the positive outcomes from providing students a variety of appropriate learning frameworks. Also in acknowledgement of the importance of learning/teaching settings, teachers, especially those in elementary schools, are committed to preparing their classrooms to make them hospitable and instructional for their students. It is my purpose to expand on these standard confirmations of the importance of *where* describing characteristics of authentic learning spaces especially as they relate to careers.

In terms of Consequential Learning, an authentic context is one in which something of value is produced by students. The old saw, *the best way to get something done is to do it,* might profitably be adapted as *the best way to learn how to do something is to do it.* This can be especially true when *the something to be done* is the production of a public outcome with acknowledged significance. In PACERS work—as referred to above—students produce newspapers, raise fish, build and monitor passive solar water heaters, and create visual and written documentation of their communities. All of them require the use and mastery of workplace concepts and tools, and in the process students are producers. It is essential to underscore here that when students are considered producers, they must also be given the responsibilities concomitant with the task. They must make critical decisions, and the possibility of failure must not be excluded from their experience. Once they become producers, students have a new self-awareness. For example students fully engaged in the newspaper project, invariably consider themselves journalists not journalism students, thus extending the old saw above to read *the best way to be a journalist is to do the work of a journalist.* Such a sense of connection often plays an important role in adolescent identity development (Erikson, 1968; Skorikov & Vondracek, 1998).

On a tour of PACERS schools, an Australian educator visited an English/Journalism classroom with me to meet with the sponsor and student staff of the community newspaper. Stopping at the door, he observed that it did not look like a classroom so much as a newspaper office. The obligatory arrangement of desks had been replaced by a variety of work stations where students were talking on phones to customers and news sources, debating the merits of a story, and completing the layout of the next edition. It was a place defined by the job to be done, and it was a place where that job could be completed. These kinds of projects, therefore, require the adaptation and/or creation of spaces where the job can get done. As a result schools and communities—with assistance from consultants—have modified existing spaces and created new ones such as aquaculture units, passive solar greenhouses, lakes, bog ponds, and newspaper labs. The spaces are often small scale models of industry settings, and can provide unique opportunities for students whose schools are not in proximity to businesses and agencies that can provide them work or study experience.

Production requires tools—good tools especially if the products are public and have recognized value. When the PACERS Community Newspaper Project (PCNP) was organized, the goal was for students to publish a local paper. Raising the bar above the publication of a school paper meant equipping young people with the tools of the industry and making sure that they understood the concepts and standards of good journalism. Therefore, the layout and design software chosen was QuarkXpress. At the time the software was the industry standard and was selected for exactly that reason. This selection had several important outcomes that might be expected whenever students are given the real "tools of the trade."

First, students, with training from professionals, are capable of using, even gaining mastery of, industry-standard tools. The expectation for them to do so is not too high, and in the case of the PCNP, even elementary students often use QuarkXpress and other high-end design software. Students' capacity with digital tools usually exceeds what teachers can do and often even what they expect. As a result students are able to take on new roles and assume responsibilities that are required by the project and which they can uniquely undertake. In this sense tools become a vehicle by which students can make clear progress in the eyes of their teachers and peers. Once the knowledge is embedded in the school it is often passed on to others by students and by teachers who have acquired the necessary skills or rebuilt with the assistance of PACERS consultants.

Second, students often respond positively to the realization that they are mastering tools used by professionals. It has not gone unnoticed to students that they are using the same design software as the *New York Times.* PCNP newspaper staffers have been called upon by local papers to teach the use of the latest software. Not only are such requests a boost to student confidence, they reconfirm the need to use the latest and best tools to position young people for entry into postsecondary work and education opportunities.

Third, almost always persons who are "outsiders" are needed to train students to use and apply the software. The "outsiders" are professionals and university journalism faculty and students. The point here goes beyond the necessary building of competence. The process introduces young people to persons engaged in or preparing for careers. It puts a face on a career, and it does so in a context in which there is a common goal that brings students and professionals together. In this process an authentic learning space is characterized by its capacity to serve as a common ground that teachers, students, professionals, and community members can occupy.

"Living labs" is a term used in PACERS projects to define contexts in which students are dealing with life and are expected to do so responsibly. Although the definition of the term is a little tautological, it emphasizes that not everything in schools that is labeled "lab" is necessarily a lab. For example most school science labs are places where the same experiments and activities are constantly repeated, and they have predictable outcomes. In comparison when students are operating an aquaculture system or writing an oral history of their community, they are responsible for the outcomes which—like life—are not predictable and require close and accurate attention. This kind of accountable attention and action parallel that of work in the real world and clearly produces habits of value. Students are willing to undertake the challenge and even raise the bar. For example, in regard to *Sunup 'til Sundown,* their oral history of agriculture on Lookout Mountain, Alabama, students at Sand Rock High School said that they were at pains "to get it perfect" because it was a record of the lives of elders in their own communities. Likewise students operating aquaculture units are appalled at the prospect of losing fish or failing to create an environment in which the fish grow in a healthy fashion. In both these examples, young people are motivated by the fact that their work has a public nature and a public benefit. People outside the school will know how they have or have not accomplished the task set before them, and students note that these kinds of projects give them the opportunity to demonstrate their competence and their interest in their communities. In this regard, students at the two schools that initiated the newspaper project cited this as a fundamental reason for being involved.

"Living lab" environments are invigorating for students who immediately distinguish such contexts from traditional school settings. This is obviously the case because the outcomes sought are not predictable and are challenging and because status based on previous grades and recognition is not automatically transferred so that new cream can rise to the top.

RELEVANT PROJECTS

Consequential Learning seeks to connect learning to place through projects and programs that are mutually beneficial to schools and communities. In order to do this most effectively, projects require a recognizable and solid relevance to local communities. The PACERS newspaper project and its science program, Rural Science for Life: Sun, Soil, and Water, are examples of relevant projects and reveal basic principles for selecting initiatives.

Student-published community newspapers are pertinent for rural communities that have no media. As rural population has declined and media has become more and more aggregated in central locations, many small rural Alabama communities have no news coverage. At the turn of the twentieth century there were more than a thousand commercial newspapers in Alabama. By the end of the century there were around one hundred. As a result for many communities there is no ongoing documentation of local life. In this situation PACERS newspapers have filled a recognized need. In some cases they have even resurrected long closed community papers, and with permission used the same name. More importantly students are media-savvy, and they understand the impact that a newspaper can have—an assessment that is continually confirmed by the response of community members to their publications.

Obviously, the choice of a local publishing project correlates immediately with a significant local need. Because of the capacity to meet a local need, predictable benefits that justify the project accrue to school and community. It is not enough that an initiative meets an important local problem. It must have academic relevance, and, in terms of career development, there should be long term implications for students. In the case of the newspapers, the process of gathering, analyzing, interpreting, and presenting information is basic for an information age. At the same time the project gives students opportunities to use digital technology— not simply do exercises but real world application. The process of publication creates a de facto computer lab with the potential for unexpected outcomes. For example, over time in the PACERS newspaper project, female students and minority students have constituted the majority of the participants. These participation rates are important because they reverse the notion that computer-related work is basically the province of males and because they reflect the high interest of minority students in technology and communications.

The project is relevant in other ways. It gives a chance for students with artistic and design skills to demonstrate what they can do. In terms of careers, this aspect of the project has provided career paths for rural Alabama students, one of whom is now a nationally recognized graphic designer employed by a major newspaper. Others have received journalism scholarships, gained employment on newspapers in Alabama and throughout the country. Others have entered related careers—especially graphic design. The point here is a simple one. There are a diversity of students and a diversity of talents in schools, and, therefore, there is a need to provide means for the expression and cultivation of a variety of interests and abilities. One teacher, discussing this point with me, told me about a student, who for four years had been the business manager of her school's paper. The student had been unsuccessful at school and generally written off but had seized the opportunity to look after the business affairs of the paper. It was a first and important step in moving to postsecondary study in business. As these various outcomes suggest, a relevant project is one that provides a wide range of learning options.

The aquaculture project's relevance is transparent to its participants, to communities, and to existing and potential partners. The U.S. has a multibillion dollar deficit in the fishing industry, and Alabama is one of the nation's most water-rich states with a climate that supports fish-growing. Therefore, the field of aquaculture is relevant and can support a variety of careers and entrepreneurial ventures. The relevance of aquaculture for economic purposes makes it a high priority in terms of education and student career preparation. However, since academic competence, interest, and success are the first order of business in Rural Science for Life, the relevance of the project for teaching and learning science is paramount. In Alabama the science component of the state's high school graduation examination concentrates upon biology, and because the aquaculture program is an immersion in basic biology, students involved in PACERS aquaculture programs have done very well (in one school with a comprehensive aquaculture program, no student failed the science component for over a decade). Without this kind of academic potential and outcome, it is difficult for educators to commit to these kinds of projects even though their value is otherwise clearly recognized and appreciated.

PACERS ongoing solar initiative demonstrates another benefit of choosing highly relevant project areas. Obviously environmental concerns and the cost of fossil fuels are generating interest in sustainable energy. That situation alone opens up the possibility for meaningful collaboration. In this case partnerships were formed with the Upper Sand Mountain Parish of the United Methodist Church and its director because of their extensive, comprehensive, and creative work in the area of passive solar design and construction—from houses to food dryers—and with retired and active engineers associated with NASA. These partners, joined by current and retired science teachers, met to consider what science subjects and contents could be taught by using passive solar devices. From that group PACERS employed consultants to work with students and to oversee related projects.

RECRUITING "OUTSIDERS"

My first rule for recruiting professional and competent local and area help is to ask. This simplistic suggestion underscores the need for the crucial and persistent activity of contacting potential partners and asking for their help. Of course asking cannot be in the abstract. By clearly defining the proposed project and the resources required, it is possible to identify what persons and/or organizations need to be contacted and what they should be asked to help with.

The second suggestion is to seek the most appropriate assistance possible. *Aim high.* When PACERS began its aquaculture program, help was sought from the Freshwater Institute (FI), a major freshwater fish research program with an interest in education. FI is located in Shepherdstown, West Virginia, and therefore was not an immediate choice. Connections were made to FI through the Lyndhurst Foundation which had been a supporter of PACERS. In the same way that students need industry standard tools, projects need the best support that they can receive. Often postsecondary institutions are prepared to provide assistance as well and are eager to do so. It is important in negotiating with agencies and institutions that the local goals and objectives are understood and that external agendas are not imposed on the project. Students recognize high quality assistance. For example in the solar project a big motivation for students has been the involvement of engineers and scientists who worked with NASA.

A third suggestion is that *help should be sought at the outset of a project.* For example in the PACERS solar project, the suggestions of engineers led to a more comprehensive program and their early ownership set the foundation for greater long term investment. Also their career knowledge and experience made clear options and benefits that would have gone unnoticed, and their enthusiasm was an important endorsement for the project goals.

Fourthly, projects should have relevance for outside organizations and professionals. For example the University of Alabama and Auburn University, public postsecondary institutions that have provided ongoing assistance for PACERS publishing projects for many years, benefit from the association. They have de facto practicums for their students, and they fulfill service obligations to the state. In the process they identify and recruit experienced and skilled students into their programs. This *mutually beneficial relationship* is likely to occur in all projects, and it underpins a stronger relationship than the usual volunteer worker situation.

PROJECTS AS PROFESSIONAL DEVELOPMENT FOR TEACHERS

The creation of authentic learning spaces for students establishes authentic teaching spaces for teachers. For example the community newspapers are a context for teaching writing, developing computer competence, and even for collecting and writing history through local community documentation.

Professional "outsiders" become colleagues with teachers and assist them to develop new skills. Professionals, as well as local community members, involved in projects tend to provide teachers important personal and vocational affirmation. The projects themselves have consequential public outcomes that bring classroom teachers a quality of recognition that cannot be provided by increasing test results.

Since PACERS projects are never undertaken only in single sites, they create opportunities for teachers in different schools to share ideas and experiences and compare outcomes. They are able to work together in developing lesson plans and other project resources. The extension of collegial associations is almost always a positive for teachers.

PROJECTS ENHANCE STUDENT LEARNING AND POTENTIAL

Case study assessments of individual projects demonstrate that these projects have several inevitable outcomes for all students' academic interest and achievement. As noted elsewhere in this chapter, the projects require skills, including ones related to critical thinking and decision making, that go beyond the normal classroom. In this context even students regarded as low achievers often come to the fore and gain recognition and affirmation. This, in turn, can and does improve their overall interest in school and their confidence in their personal capacity. It has often been the case in PACERS work that students without standing or interest in school acquire that combination of capacity and confidence necessary to pursue successfully career options.

The prospect of improved academic interest and achievement is enhanced by the opportunity for the practical application of what is being taught in the classroom. For example, I have been told repeatedly by science teachers that their students could not explain pH until they went to work in their aquaculture unit where the relevance of pH was tied to the survival of the fish. Newspapers are written for an audience, and the audience—especially because it is valued by students—evokes greater commitment to getting things right. For example, one student explained that she had never considered the purpose for a comma until she wrote for the newspaper. Then she had to get it right because her grandmother would be reading her articles and discussing them with her neighbors.

In these projects young people get a taste of real world applications of what they are learning. This contrasts vividly with the increasing notion that learning is for the purpose of testing, and that may mean simply the accumulation of bits and pieces of disposable information. Now they can actually see evidence of what they learn in school and how it might be applied. In addition the contexts provide teachers new options for strengthening students' commitment to learning.

Through the projects students create outcomes that attract positive attention for themselves and for the school. Simply accomplishing something worthwhile gives energy to those involved, and when there is external affirmation, that energy and pride level is compounded.

ORGANIZING LOCAL COMMUNITY SUPPORT

Local community support of these kinds of initiatives is crucial in several ways. In the projects described in this chapter, local communities contribute money, skilled labor/expertise, and materials. No project receives PACERS support without a signed agreement between PACERS, the school, and the PACERS chapter (for details on project and local chapter requirements see *www.pacersinc.org*). Because of the relevance of the projects, local people are usually eager to help, and because of the specific nature of the projects, they are able to contribute. For example, in the aquaculture programs, local people, businesses, and legislative representatives have assisted with everything from helping to prepare building and pond sites to giving funds and construction materials. Local people with aquaculture skills help maintain facilities. In the solar project, local carpenters and plumbers assist with the construction of passive solar water heaters and greenhouses. Their contribution of time and skill are essential and are to be sought even when there are funds available to contract all work. As with the aquaculture program, an inevitable outcome is local ownership in the project and consequently in the school. This ownership based on contributions to and intimate knowledge of the projects is essential for sustaining projects especially when there are changes in teachers and/or administrators.

Community members also have the opportunity to build their own capacity to assist with projects. For example, scholarships are made available by PACERS for community members to attend aquaculture courses at Gadsden State Community College and local solar workshops are held to assist local project supporters to understand better the goals and needs of the project. The projects are naturally an important local learning resource.

Local relationships to projects are formalized in agreement forms that are signed by community members and specify their responsibilities which include an end of the year documentation of the project. Such clarity and accountability are central to making partnerships work (Hands, this volume). Local PACERS groups set up the context in which teachers and students involved in the project are interviewed as part of PACERS documentation process (information on the interview process is available from *admin@pacersinc.org*). This process extends local knowledge of the outcomes of the project for students and teachers, creates an opportunity for discussing means for improving and better resourcing projects, is a context in which young people can be recognized, and develops information essential for interpretation and fund raising.

Local engagement in the school around important activities is a byproduct of community support for these projects. In these processes there is interaction between students and adults—an interaction that is almost always missing in contemporary schooling and that is vital for students' personal growth and preparation for their lives beyond school. The disconnect between students and adults is grounded in the growing separation between schools and communities, a division that is a major cause of concern about the future of public engagement in public education. Outside of extracurricular activities, especially athletics, there are few means by which local communities can participate in or have a sense of ownership of their schools. These projects can help fill the gap.

NECESSITIES AND IMPEDIMENTS

Decades of this work have clarified a few basic and seemingly predictable essentials for and obstacles to its success. The first essential is a recognition that young people can and will undertake challenging work that benefits their communities. This awareness has two components. First, students are talented and intelligent and capable of meeting the challenge of demanding work. Second, they are motivated by projects connected to the well-being of their communities and within which they gain local recognition. There is no greater impediment than a negative assessment of students' ability and commitment. I have found that even teachers who begin with a positive assessment often comment that their students exceeded all their expectations.

This "first essential" is important for the obvious reason that a project cannot be undertaken in good faith without interest from its major players. It also prepares the way for students to take significant roles in the project. Without confidence in them, they will not be allowed to be the critical decision makers. A good rule of thumb in this regard was set by a PACERS aquaculture sponsor at Florala High School who gave his students 90% of all decision making relevant to the life of the fish. This of course led to some dead fish, but it also was fundamental for students' understanding of their responsibilities and for their ability to fulfill them and to deal with the consequences of failing to do so.

PACERS projects place students in the central role. They are the publishers, builders, aqua-scientists, and so forth. As such their relationship to teachers and professionals often moves toward being a collegial one. This shift is noted by teachers with enthusiasm because it represents growth in student capacity and self-understanding, and clear movement toward postsecondary success.

Project success is almost always dependent upon competent, imaginative, and committed teachers who are supported by the school administration and by "outsiders" including the community, professionals, and related organizations. In the case of PACERS, the organization seeks to further support teachers by connecting them to each other in workshops and in contexts in which they develop curriculum and other project support materials. Teachers also are provided stipends for attending related continuing education classes such as the aquaculture classes provided by Gadsden State Community College, and for preparing lesson plans. Backup by professionals is often critical—not only at the start of a project—but in order for teachers to maximize project potential and to imagine and plan for its further development.

Teachers and principals may be reticent to undertake projects because they do not see their application to their existing responsibilities or priorities. Some teachers want to do this kind of work but cannot immediately grasp its relevance. To address this question, it is often necessary to have support materials—for example, a comprehensive collection of lesson plans with crossovers to state requirements clearly articulated (an example of such a collection prepared for the PACERS solar science project is available at cost by contacting *admin@pacersinc.org*), and documentation that records the perspectives and success of former participants.

On the impediment list, there is the ongoing divide in schools between what might be called academic and technical or classroom and shop. In this context, technical and shop seem often to be written off as the province of students who cannot learn. Unfortunately, this may preclude the opportunity for students with postsecondary aspirations to learn by doing and block educators' capacity to understand the academic potential in projects with strong technical components. There also appears to be a growing disinterest in providing students the opportunity to work with their hands and to learn particular skills—even those that are clearly related to academic achievement as measured by test scores. These factors come into play with projects like those described in this chapter, and always necessitate constant reiteration of the academic benefits such as improved test scores and of student interest.

The status given to standardized testing is unmatched in the history of American education. Many teachers administrators, along with their controlling education departments and boards, are so dominated by it that test-taking preparation is usually the only order of the day. This is a dulling down of teaching and perhaps of the teaching profession itself. It can and does stifle individual teacher initiative, insight, and even commitment. Therefore, in many cases the question becomes "what is the relevance of the proposed project to test scores?" This is a very limited question and very disappointing when it is the only question that matters enough to be considered. Examples of PACERS impact on scores—such as the science graduation scores mentioned above—are provided for principals. However, it is usually the case that principals quickly see the value of PACERS, and if they do not it is difficult for them to be persuaded. At the same time, administrators can use preparation for testing as an excuse for avoiding the development of new initiatives no matter their potential benefits to students and communities.

Schooling is increasingly standardized and professionalized and power is likewise being more and more centralized. The process tends to dampen the attention, capacity, and willingness of schools to connect to communities or to organizations and people outside the educational silo. Communities are not the subject of study, and generally they are not considered to be resources. Community connection, support, and interaction are basic to the Consequential Learning approach. On occasion, it conflicts directly with the assumption or presumption that communities have no business inside schools and should fulfill their main function which is to pay the taxes.

SUMMARY OF CAREER IMPLICATIONS FROM THE CONSEQUENTIAL LEARNING APPROACH

Valuable connections, with both short and long term implications, are made through the kinds of projects undertaken in the Consequential Learning approach. For young people, associations are made in a work environment with professionals, postsecondary students, organizations, and educational institutions. These associations provide insights into careers and the pathways that lead to them. For teachers, collegial relationships with professionals and postsecondary representatives are often formed and new perspectives on and links to career options are gained. Also, the projects provide professionals and organizations opportunities to engage with schools with the outcomes usually confirming the mutually beneficial nature of the partnerships formed.

For students in rural Alabama schools, these kinds of projects provide work experience that may not be accessible to them due to distance or simply to the lack of businesses in the area. The experience is not that of a single student being assigned to an internship but of entire classes working together, and it is an experience in which young people are expected to fill all the roles. Sustained engagement in productive activity is among the most important factors in preparing students for a satisfying work life (Czikszentmihalyi & Schneider, 2000). Furthermore, on a very practical level, their experiences can be added to their resumes, and it will be useful to them in interview situations.

In order to fill the full range of positions required to complete the project, students must use—perhaps even master— the requisite tools and concepts. Of course, gaining a broad range of skills is an outcome, and in addition students often build de facto portfolios (such as newspapers that they helped publish).

The experience of teachers should not be overlooked. The projects link them as well to persons and organizations that can and do provide new and better options for their students. This kind of experience may be common for counselors and for persons in technical schools, but it is not for other teachers. In this context—they, like their students—get a better grasp on where their instruction of students is leading.

Student mastery of career relevant skills and concepts is probably the most significant expectation and outcome of this approach and the projects through which it is implemented. There is nothing that can move young people further toward success than competence in using the tools and practices of a profession. With the successful—and in this case, public—application of tools and concepts come essential personal confidence and the recognition of that competence by others including employers and representatives of postsecondary institutions.

REFERENCES

Czikszentmihalyi, M. & Schneider, B. (2000). *Becoming adult.* New York: Basic Books.

Erikson, E., (1968). Youth, identity, and crisis. New York: Norton.

National Commission on the High School Senior (2001). *Youth at the crossroads; Facing high school and beyond.* Washington DC: The Education Trust.

PACERS (2007). Welcome to PACERS. Retrieved October 19, 2008 from www.pacersinc.org

Shelton, J. (2005). *Consequential Learning,* Montgomery AL: New South Books. Skorikov, V. & Vondracedk, F. W. (1998). Vocational identity development: Its relationship to other identity domains and overall identity development. *Journal of Career Assessment, 6*(1), 13–35.

CHAPTER 8

EMERGING STATE POLICIES AND PROGRAMS DESIGNED TO SUPPORT PARENTAL INVOLVEMENT IN POSTSECONDARY PLANNING

Jennifer Dounay Zinth

While increasing numbers of students believe they will go to college, many youth and their parents do not receive the information they need to achieve this goal. This paper examines statistics comparing students' educational aspirations to postsecondary attainment; highlights economic projections of the need for postsecondary credentials among members of the future workforce; reviews research on the important role parents play in college planning, preparation, and selection; and offers an overview of state policies intended to help ensure all parents and students—and particularly first-generation college-goers—receive the information and support they need. Such policies address college entrance expectations, goal-setting and course selection, annual updates on student progress toward graduation

Promising Practices for Family and Community Involvement during High School, pages 121–137

goals, and information on completing college admissions and financial aid applications.

Bronfenbrenner's (1979) ecological paradigm provides a theoretical framework that connects how individual students, their parents, classrooms, and peers influence and are influenced by the expectations, aspirations, information, and messages about postsecondary education in both the proximal and distal environment. Broad societal factors like race, culture, and economics also impact postsecondary planning and attainment. Bronfenbrenner further suggest that policy made at both the exo and macro system levels impacts students and their families by shaping opportunities and access available to them in their schools and communities.

College Aspirations

National, state, and local surveys are all in agreement: The vast majority of high school students state the belief that they will go to college. A nationwide 2006 survey reported that 83% of white students, 72% of black students, and 59% of Hispanic students said they are "definitely going to college" (Public Agenda, 2006). In another nationwide survey, 75% of youths age 13–19 said they planned to attend a four-year institution, while an additional 18% planned to continue to a two-year institution or training/vocational program (Horatio Alger Association). Three out of four high school students surveyed nationally in 2006 responded, when asked why they go to school, "Because I want to get a degree and go to college"—the most common response to this question (Yazzie-Mintz, 2007). Nearly eight out of 10 of West Virginia's Class of 2007—including more than 70% of low-income and first-generation college-goers—said they hoped to earn at least a bachelor's degree (Ness, 2007). Similarly, Indiana's 2007–2008 Career and College Information Survey, an annual survey of ninth and eleventh graders in the state, found that 83% of the Class of 2009 expect to earn either a two- or four-year college degree (De Witt, Hansen, & Rinkenberger, 2008). Just 6% believe their education will stop with a high school diploma (De Witt et al., 2008). Additionally, a 2005 survey of Chicago high school seniors indicated that 78% aspired to completing a bachelor's degree or higher, while 14% hoped to earn vocational certification or a two-year degree (Roderick et al., 2006).

Parents and members of the general public likewise feel going to college is important. A 2007 survey of parents of middle grades students found 87% believed their child would go to college; less than 1% thought their child would not (Cunningham, Erisman, & Looney, 2007). A whopping 96% of 1,054 Latino parents in a 2002 survey expected their child to go to college (Tornatzky, Cutler, & Lee, 2002). Three in four parents in a 2007 poll said a college education was needed to succeed in the modern world (Cunningham et al., 2007). Similarly, a 2003 nationwide survey of adults found that nearly eight in ten Americans feel "having a college degree is more important for economic success today than it was 20 or 30 years ago. Two-thirds (67%) believe it is a *lot* more important" (Lake Snell Perry & Associates, Inc., 2003).

The percentage of high school students who plan to complete a bachelor's degree or higher has increased in recent years. From 1980 to 2002, the number of tenth graders who planned to complete their education at the bachelor's degree level leaped from 23% to 40%; those planning to finish their education at the graduate/first professional degree level more than doubled over the same period, from 18% to 40% (Calahan et al., 2006). These aspirations rose among students in all socioeconomic status (SES) levels, but the greatest gain was in bachelor's degree aspirations among students in the lowest quarter SES. Even between 2001 and 2005, the Horatio Alger study found the percentage of youth reporting no plans to attend college slipped from 5% to 3%; the number setting their sights on a four-year institution rose nearly 10 points, from 68% to 76% (2005).

Recent surveys suggest that students begin developing opinions on whether or not they will attend college as early as the middle grades (Markow, Liebman, & Dunbar, 2007; Ness, 2007). Ninety-two percent of participants in a 2007 survey of U.S. students in grades 7 and 8 responded that they believed they would go to college (Markow et al., 2007).

Economic projections support this emphasis on college completion. According to the Bureau of Labor Statistics, 22 of the 30 fastest-growing jobs between 2006 and 2016 will require some postsecondary credential—be it technical certification, a two- or four-year degree, professional degree, or a master's degree (2006). And the U.S. Chamber of Commerce (2007) suggests that nine out of 10 of the fastest-growing jobs will require some form of postsecondary education.

College Attendance

However, statistics suggest that many students' (and their parents') aspirations for college are not realized. The National Center for Higher Education Management Systems [NCHEMS], factoring in student attrition during high school, suggests that nationwide, only 38% of students entering grade nine will have entered college by age nineteen (with delay of college entry for more than one year after high school completion associated with a decreased likelihood of postsecondary completion) (NCHEMS, 2002). Other research suggests that fewer than half of high school *graduates* in 10 states enter postsecondary education within a year of leaving high school,

(NCHEMS and Jobs for the Future, 2007). Allensworth, as cited by Roderick (2006), reported that minority youth who hope to complete a four-year degree are more likely to end up matriculating in a two-year institution or not entering postsecondary education at all. This gives broader context to the Roderick (2006) finding that in Chicago, a district with a significant minority student population, while the vast majority of the 92% of high school seniors with postsecondary ambitions planned to earn a bachelor's degree or higher, only 13 of the district's 74 high schools sent more than 50% of their graduates to a four-year institution. Data are not currently available on the transition rates of Chicago high school graduates from two- to four-year postsecondary institutions.

Some forecasts suggest that U.S. economic competitiveness will be challenged by an insufficient number of degree holders, meaning that inadequate postsecondary attainment has implications for not only individual students and their families, but communities, states, and the nation as a whole (Santiago, 2006).

The disparity between stated postsecondary goals and actual postsecondary attainment is even more troubling given the commonly agreed-upon benefits of completing postsecondary education. The Institute for Higher Education Policy (as cited by the Social Science Research Council, 2005), has developed a matrix of the economic and social benefits to society as well as the individual when students earn a college degree (Table 8.1).

So, given the high aspirations of many students (and their parents), the projections of the growing need for a more educated workforce to meet future labor market needs, the potential challenge to America's economic competitiveness due to an inadequate supply of postsecondary degree-

TABLE 8.1 The Array of Benefits to Higher Education

	Public	Private
Economic	• Increased Tax Revenues • Greater Productivity • Increased Consumption • Increased Workforce Flexibility • Decreased Reliance on Government Financial Support	• Higher Salaries and Benefits • Employment • Higher Savings Levels • Improved Working Conditions • Personal/Professional Mobility
Social	• Reduced Crime Rates • Increased Charitable Giving/Community Service • Increased Quality of Civic Life • Social Cohesion/Appreciation of Diversity • Improved Ability to Adapt to and Use Technology	• Improved Health/Life Expectancy • Improved Quality of Life for Offspring • Better Consumer Decision-making • Increased Personal Status • More Hobbies, Leisure Activities

holders, and the commonly-known public and private benefits of completing a postsecondary education, why do more students not enter college? Many sources suggest that a simple lack of knowledge of college admission expectations, college costs, and financial aid opportunities is at least partially to blame—and that non-honors track, first-generation, low-income, and minority students and their parents are most likely to be lacking this key information (Venezia & Kirst 2005; Antonio & Bersola, 2004; Venezia, Kirst, & Antonio 2003; National Postsecondary Education Cooperative [NPEC] 2007; Tornatzky et al., 2002).

College Preparation and Planning

The literature on college preparation and application typically refers to a three-part process defined by Hossler (as cited by the NPEC, 2007). The "predisposition" stage is a period of self-reflection during which the individual decides to pursue postsecondary education. "Individual and environmental background factors have the strongest influence at this stage, informing one's self-image, preferences, and inclinations" (NPEC, 2007). During the "search" stage, individuals seek information about college choices. At the beginning of this stage, students are most influenced by social networks, but institutions have greater influence as this stage progresses. Lastly, in the "choice" stage, students and their families sort through the gathered information "within the context of their personal and social circumstances, resulting in decisions about whether to apply to college, which colleges to apply to, and which college to attend" (NPEC, 2007). At all three stages, students and their parents are influenced by messages they receive from others.

At each stage of the college planning and selection process, research makes clear that parents play a vital role in helping their children set their sights on, prepare for, and attend college. Findings (Antonio & Bersola, 2004; Merchant 2004; Bueschel & Venezia, 2004; NPEC 2007) suggest that high school students of all income and racial groups are typically more likely to seek college guidance from their parents than from counselors, teachers, or other sources. Cabrera and La Nasa (2000) propose that parental encouragement and involvement directly and strongly influence their child's early and later educational and career aspirations, college qualifications, and, ultimately, their child's college choice. Choy, Horn, Nuñez, and Chen (2000) found that at-risk students and those whose parents did not attend college were almost twice as likely to enroll in a four-year postsecondary education if their parents frequently talked to them about school-related matters, in comparison to their peers whose parents had discussed these topics infrequently or not at all. In an analysis of the respective roles of parents and counselors, McDonough (2005) notes that "parents participated in their children's college-choice processes through encouragement, involvement, and as knowledge providers and interpreters and that counselors' major work with parents was to provide them with informational materials and meetings" (as cited in McDonough 1997).

PREPARATION FOR POSTSECONDARY EDUCATION DURING HIGH SCHOOL

Information Parents and Students Need

However, little attention has been paid to the policy and programmatic approaches states have recently begun to adopt in an effort to (1) provide parents with accurate information on postsecondary options and costs, and (2) provide structured guidance to parents and students as they proceed through the college planning and selection process. State policy can in turn influence district- and school-level policy, to ensure that all parents and students receive essential information that will enhance parents' ability to provide the college guidance for which their children turn to them. The author's synthesis of various sources (Cunningham et al., 2007; Venezia & Kirst 2005; Antonio & Bersola 2004; Venezia 2004; Merchant 2004; Bueschel & Venezia 2004; Kirst, Venezia, & Antonio 2004; Venezia, Kirst, & Antonio 2003; NPEC 2007; Tornatzky et al., 2002; Markow et al., 2007) suggests that more students—particularly traditionally underserved students—might complete high school and successfully transition to postsecondary if states provided all high school students and parents with the following: (1) Information on college entrance expectations, such as minimum course requirements, grade point average, and so forth; (2) Guidance on setting post-high school goals and annually selecting high school courses to achieve those goals; (3) Annual updates on students' progress toward graduation goals; (4) Information on and guidance in completing college and financial aid applications.

This chapter highlights state approaches intended to ensure that students and their parents receive the information they need at each step of the college planning process to make well-informed decisions. First, I will describe state policies that require all students and parents to receive advance notification or "signaling" of admissions requirements at four-year postsecondary institutions in the state. Next, I will set forth examples of state policies to help students and parents set goals for high school completion and college entry, and select the high school courses that will place students on the path to achieve those secondary and postsecondary goals. I will then identify state policies that keep parents informed of students' progress toward high school completion goals, given the relationship between high school graduation and entry into postsecondary education, particularly into four-year degree programs. I will subsequently describe state approaches to provide students and parents with the information and guidance they may need as they select a college and complete college admissions applications. Lastly, I will set forth means states are using to ensure all students and parents receive accurate information on college costs and financial aid.

Providing Information on College Entrance Expectations

Despite the important role parents play in setting academic expectations for their children, and the fact that students must take certain courses in high school to be eligible for admission to four-year postsecondary institutions, research suggests that parents are often unaware of the courses required for college entry (Antonio & Bersola, 2004, Merchant, 2004, Bueschel & Venezia, 2004). Colorado is one of the rare states that requires all students and their parents to be notified of the course admissions requirements common to all public four-year institutions in the state. Legislation directs the Colorado commission on higher education to annually mail to all parents of public school eighth-graders the commission's "admission guidelines and an explanation that compliance with the higher education admission guidelines is necessary for acceptance, but is not a guarantee of admission, to a state-supported institute of higher education" (COLO. REV. STAT. ANN. § 23-1-119.1(1)(a); Colorado Department of Higher Education Policies and Procedures (I)(F)(4.00). To avoid potential confusion that students not meeting the guidelines will be barred from admission, the notice must also explain the potential need for remediation and related financial costs if a student seeks access to a commission-governed postsecondary institution but does not meet the recommended guidelines (COLO. REV. STAT. ANN. § 23-1-119.1(1)(b)). South Dakota goes a step further, requiring the board of regents to *annually* inform parents of grade 7–12 students "about the courses needed to prepare for postsecondary-level work and about the benefits of such preparation" (S.D. Codified Laws § 13-28-50).

Texas is the first of a growing number of states to apply a slightly different approach. While the state does not have common admissions requirements to four-year public postsecondary institutions, it has established a "Recommended" curriculum that is in keeping with four-year postsecondary admissions requirements in many states. This "Recommended" curriculum, required as the default high school curriculum beginning with the Class of 2008, includes four years English; three years mathematics in a sequence of Algebra I, geometry, Algebra II; three years science; four years social sciences; and two years foreign language (TEX. EDUC. CODE ANN. § 25.025(a); 19 TEX. ADMIN. CODE § 74.53). In addition, legislation directs all counselors in elementary and middle/junior high schools to "advise students and their parents or guardians regarding the importance of higher education, [and] coursework designed to prepare students for higher education" (TEX. EDUC. CODE ANN. § 33.007(a)). In a student's first and senior years of high school, counselors must provide students and their parents with information on "the importance of higher education" and "the advantages of completing the recommended or advanced high school program" (TEX. EDUC. CODE ANN. § 33.007(b)(1-2). Legislation likewise requires each district's district improvement plan to include strategies for informing middle and high school students—and their parents, teachers and counselors—about higher education admissions (TEX. EDUC. CODE ANN. § 11.252(a)(4)(A)).

Setting Goals and Choosing High School Courses

As indicated by Cabrera and La Nasa (2000) (adapted from Nora and Cabrera, 1992), "parental support and encouragement" are key in the late middle grades and first years of high school, as students begin to develop career and educational aspirations and enroll in college-prep courses. While one analysis of NCES National Education Longitudinal Study of 1988 (NELS:88) data suggests a surprising number of high school dropouts—43%—eventually enroll in some form of postsecondary education (Hurst, Kelly, & Princiotta, 2005), research indicates even those dropouts who eventually earn a GED are less likely to complete some form of postsecondary education than their peers who earned a high school diploma (Laird, DeBell, Kienzl, & Chapman 2007; Tyler 2002). Young dropouts surveyed cite a disconnect between course material and the "real world," boredom, and being held to low expectations as the main reasons for leaving school (Bridgeland, DiIulio, & Morison, 2006).

Individual graduation plans or learning plans for all students are one means to help students set post-high school goals and commit to completing the courses that will improve their chances of a successful post-high school transition, regardless of whether that transition is to postsecondary education or to the workforce. As of February 2008, 21 states and the District of Columbia either require or will require all students to develop an individual graduation plan (Dounay, 2007a). In the majority of these states, the individual graduation plan (referred to in some jurisdictions as the "individual learning plan") is jointly developed in grade eight by the student, the student's parent, and a guidance counselor, and establishes the courses a student will complete each year of high school to be prepared for the student's stated goal of college or workforce entry. Typically, the plan is annually reviewed by the student, parent, and counselor, and changes are made based on shifts in the student's postsecondary and/or career goals. Some states also require the plan to include extracurricular activities that will assist the student in achieving post-high school goals; some states explicitly require the plan to include the year after the student's graduation from high school. A small number of states require structured college and career planning to begin even earlier than grade eight. For example, Kentucky legislation mandates that, effective with the Class of 2013, development of each student's individual learning plan must begin as early as grade six (704 KY. ADMIN. REGS. 3:305).

As of February 2008, state policies in at least four states—Indiana (Class of 2011), South Dakota (Class of 2010), Oklahoma (Class of 2010), and Ohio (Class of 2014) (with a small number of exceptions)—will require all high school students to complete graduation requirements aligned with the courses required for unconditional freshman admission to public four-year institutions in the state (Dounay 2006; OHIO REV. CODE ANN. § 3345.06(B)). Such policies address the "signaling" of post-high school expectations that Venezia and Kirst (2005) suggest can help students and their parents receive clear messages about college expectations.

In these and most other states like Texas that require a rigorous default high school curriculum, the individual graduation plan is essentially an agreement that the student will complete the curriculum. Plans typically require that if the student elects to complete a lower-level curriculum, the student and the student's parent must be informed of the potential negative educational and/or economic consequences of selecting the lower-level curriculum (Dounay 2007).

Providing Annual Updates on Student Progress

Simply setting goals will not ensure that students make steady progress toward achieving them—or that parents will be kept informed of their child's academic progress. Bridgeland and colleagues (2006) found that the majority of recent dropouts' parents were "not aware" or only "somewhat aware" of their children's grades and attendance. Dropouts themselves in the Bridgeland and colleagues study suggested that better communication between school and home would improve young people's likelihood of staying in school. Relatively few states appear to have adopted policies requiring parents to be notified of their child's progress toward completing high school graduation requirements. One exception, Iowa, requires districts to annually report to each student (and each minor student's parent) the student's progress in completing state high school graduation requirements (IOWA CODE ANN. § 279.61). Likewise, Washington State requires high schools to annually send the parents of students grades 9–12 the graduation requirements applicable to their child at the beginning of the school year, and at school year's end, their child's progress toward completing those requirements. The high school of any student "not making normal progress" toward completion of those requirements must notify the student and parent "of alternative education experiences, including summer school opportunities available in the community, if any, or in close proximity" (WASH. ADMIN. CODE § 180-51-045).

Selecting a College and Completing College Applications

While research indicates that students look to their parents for help in searching for colleges and completing applications for admission, studies also indicate parents of low-income and first-generation college students are less well-equipped or less likely to assist in such activities (NPEC, 2007, Choy, 2001, Choy et al., 2000). Choy found that first-generation college-goers were no more likely to receive help at school with the college application process than students of parents who attended college. These findings suggest that low-income and first generation students and their parents "would benefit from additional information and resources and from assistance in interpreting and using information" to help them complete college applications (NPEC, 2007). In a similar vein, Venezia and Kirst (2005) noted that students "wanted educators to go through the materials with them—not just hand them information without walking them through it, step-by-step" (2005).

To address the need for personalized guidance through the college search and application process, Texas has launched an effort that is quite possibly the only state approach of its kind nationwide. As part of the College for Texans Campaign, the state is making available a statewide web of locally-based centers, dubbed "Go Centers," to offer students and their parents information about colleges and guidance in selecting a college. "Traditional" Go Centers are primarily based on high school campuses, but can also be found on middle school or postsecondary campuses; "satellite" Go Centers have been established in locations such as public libraries, community centers. and local workforce centers (Go Center Manual, n.d.). All Go Centers offer a "Go Center Sponsor," a trained adult whose duties include helping students research postsecondary, career and financial aid options, and computers with Internet access to allow students and parents to browse online resources. "Collegiate G-Force" chapters, Go Centers established on over 60 postsecondary campuses in the state, also offer outreach to high schools, as well as opportunities for college students to mentor high school students through the college selection process (Go Center Manual, n.d.). In addition, Mobile Go Centers, based out of four Texas colleges and universities, are vans equipped with computers with high-speed Internet connections, "designed to bring college-related information, motivation, and assistance to students and their families" ("Mobile Go Center," 2006a and 2006b). The Austin Community College Mobile Go Center "stops at schools, shopping malls, community centers, and other locations" to support students and families in the college decision-making process ("Welcome to," n.d.).

Completing college applications can be a daunting prospect, particularly to students whose parents did not attend college or whose parents' low English proficiency limits their capacity to help their child. States are just beginning to develop policies to guide students in completing college application forms and in simplifying the college application process. For example, Texas has developed a Common Application, with instructions in both English and Spanish, accepted by all public four-year institutions in the state, as well as ApplyTexas, a free Web site through which students may submit their application to any public four-year institution in the state, and to some two-year and private institutions (ApplyTexas.org, n.d.; 2007–2008 Texas Common Application, 2007). The aforementioned Go Centers are equipped with shelves stocked with the Texas Common Application and community college applications (Go Center Manual, n.d.).

Indiana is one of a small number of states that has developed an e-transcript system allowing students to easily send transcripts online (Indiana e-Transcript a, n.d.). The Web site for high school counselors makes clear the benefits of this service to students and parents: "Students gain the convenience of online transcript requesting and tracking; automatic notifications are provided from request through delivery" (Indiana e-Transcript b, n.d.). The financial benefits to students and families—particularly low-income families—are also clear: "With a statewide average of each student requesting six transcripts, the savings adds up to over $40 per typical college-bound student" (Indiana e-Transcript c, n.d.).

Communicating Key Information on College Costs and Financial Aid

Low-income parents cite data about college costs and financial aid as most important in their college searches, more important than information about majors/programs of study or admissions requirements (NPEC, 2007). Information about college costs also appears to be more important to low-income parents than to their children (NPEC, 2007). Students and parents often overestimate the cost of postsecondary tuition, while some students erroneously believe ability-to-pay is a factor in college admissions (Antonio & Bersola, 2004; Venezia, 2004; Merchant, 2004; Bueschel & Venezia, 2004; Turner, Jones & Hearn, 2004; Mintrop, Milton, Schmidtlein & MacLellan, 2004; Venezia, Kirst, & Antonio, 2003; NPEC, 2007; Markow et al., 2007, Ness, 2007). Collectively, these factors and misperceptions of college costs can negatively influence students' decision to attend college (NPEC, 2007; Markow et al., 2007, Ness, 2007; Merchant, 2004; Kirst, Venezia, & Antonio, 2004). NPEC research likewise suggests that while key information about college costs is often available through Web sites and other sources, this information is "less accessible" (because there is no Internet connection at home) or "less comprehensible—especially cost, financial aid, and scholarship information—for underserved students than for middle income students" (NPEC, 2007). Furthermore, the Stanford Bridge Project found that "I have to be a stellar athlete or student to get financial aid" is one of the "top ten myths" students believe about college (Kirst, Venezia, & Antonio, 2004; Venezia, Kirst, & Antonio, 2003).

Texas is the only state that addresses this information gap by requiring all elementary, middle and senior high school counselors to advise students on financial aid eligibility requirements. And when counselors provide all students and their parents with information on higher education during students' first and senior year of high school (as mentioned above under "College Entrance Expectations"), they must also include information about financial aid eligibility, instruction on how to apply for federal financial aid, and the state's "center for financial aid information" (TEX. EDUC. CODE ANN. § 33.007(b)(4–6). This center, known as the Texas Financial Aid Information Center, maintains a toll-free hotline staffed by "real people" (callers during operational hours do not reach a phone tree or prerecorded messages) who can provide students and parents with financial aid information. English/Spanish bilingual staffers are available (page 2, "College Planning Guide," n.d.).

Research has also suggested that the complexity of the Free Application for Federal Student Aid (FAFSA) form, a requirement for the Pell Grant and for many state-level scholarships, may deter some students and families from completing the application (Dynarski & Scott-Clayton, 2006; Advisory Committee on Student Financial Assistance, 2005). This complexity may be an obstacle in particular to those in greatest need—low-income families, who are more likely to be first generation college-goers or speakers of a language other than English at home (Dynarski & Scott-Clayton, 2006). And in fact, from 1999–2000 to 2003–2004, the proportion of undergraduates who did not fill out the FAFSA increased from 50% to 59%; the number of these undergraduates who were from low- and middle-income families increased from 1.7 million to 1.8 million (American Council on Education, 2006).

States have begun to require high schools to offer structured opportunities for students and families to receive assistance in completing the FAFSA. In a unique approach, Tennessee legislation requires every high school to conduct workshops for students in grades 10–12 and their parents on completing college admission and financial aid applications, with special emphasis on providing guidance to high school seniors and their parents. Districts, in turn, must annually report to the state department of education "when each school conducted college admissions workshops, the number of students participating, the percentage of students participating in each grade and the activities that occurred at such workshops." These data are to be evaluated by the department and submitted in an annual report to the state senate and house education committees (TENN. CODE ANN. § 49-4-932, (g) & (i). Alternatively, the aforementioned Texas Go Centers are encouraged to host financial aid nights in February, to offer students and parents help with completing the FAFSA. The Go Center Manual indicates that all Go Centers should be equipped with FAFSA forms, as well as Internet-connected computers for students to complete the FAFSA application online. The timeline in the Go Center Manual urges Go Center staff to touch base with seniors in February, to make sure they've submitted the FAFSA. While Go Centers encourage students to complete the FAFSA online, they maintain copies of the FAFSA in both English and Spanish for students to take home to complete beforehand (Go Center Manual, n.d.).

CONCLUSION

The policy approaches described here have not been evaluated for impact on student college-going because (1) the state policy approaches described here are relatively new, and/or (2) K–12 and postsecondary student data systems in many states do not make it possible to determine the percentage of high school graduates who enroll in college within a year of high school graduation (Data Quality Campaign, n.d.). Future research on the impact of such policies might survey students (who did and did not attend college) and their parents on whether the information they received was helpful. Researchers should also ask about the type of information families did not receive but would have considered valuable. Lastly, researchers could (or should) survey students and their parents as to whether receipt of college preparation information ultimately influenced students' decisions related to attending and paying for college.

REFERENCES

American Council on Education. (2006). *Missed Opportunities Revisited: New Information on Students Who Do Not Apply for Financial Aid.* Washington, DC: Author.

Antonio, A. L., & Bersola, S. H. (2004). Working Toward K–16 Coherence in California. In Kirst, M.W., & Venezia, A. (Eds.), *From High School to College: Improving Opportunities for Success in Postsecondary Education* (pp. 31–76). San Francisco: Jossey-Bass.

ApplyTexas.org. (n.d.). Retrieved February 29, 2008 from https://www.applytexas.org/adappc/gen/c_start.WBX

Arbona, C., & Nora, A. (2007). The Influence of Academic and Environmental Factors on Hispanic College Degree Attainment. *The Review of Higher Education, volume 30,* (Spring 2007), pp. 247–269.

Bridgeland, J. M., DiIulio, J. J. Jr., Morison, K. B. (2006). *The Silent Epidemic: Perspectives of High School Dropouts.* Retrieved February 27, 2008 from http://www.gatesfoundation.org/nr/downloads/ed/TheSilentEpidemic3-06FINAL.pdf.

Bronfenbrenner, U. (1979). *The ecology of human development: Experiments by nature and design.* Cambridge: MA: Harvard University Press.

Bueschel, A. C., & Venezia, A. (2004). Oregon's K–16 Reforms. In Kirst, M.W., & Venezia, A. (Eds.), *From High School to College: Improving Opportunities for Success in Postsecondary Education* (pp. 151–182). San Francisco: Jossey-Bass.

Bureau of Labor Statistics. *Table 6: The 30 fastest-growing occupations, 2006–2016.* Retrieved February 25, 2008 from http://www.bls.gov/news.release/ecopro.t06.htm./

Cabrera, A. F., & La Nasa, S. M. (2000). Understanding the College-Choice Process. In A. F. Cabrera & S. M. La Nasa (Ed.), *Understanding the College Choice of Disadvantaged Students* (pp. 5–22). San Francisco: Jossey-Bass Publishers.

Cahalan, M. W., Ingels, S.J., Burns, L. J., Planty, M., and Daniel, B. (2006). *United States High School Sophomores: A Twenty-Two Year Comparison, 1980–2002* (NCES 2006-327). U.S. Department of Education. Washington, DC: National Center for Education Statistics.

Choy, S. P., Horn, L. J., Nuñez, A.-M.. & Chen, X. (2000). Transition to College: What Helps At-Risk Students and Students Whose Parents Did Not Attend College. In A. F. Cabrera & S. M. La Nasa (Eds.), *Understanding the College Choice of Disadvantaged Students* (pp. 45–63). San Francisco: Jossey-Bass Publishers.

College Planning Guide. (n.d.). Retrieved February 28, 2008, from http://www.collegefortexans.com/Publications/CollegePlanningGuide.pdf

Cunningham, A., Erisman, W., & Looney, S. M. (2007). *From Aspirations to Action: The Role of Middle School Parents in Making the Dream of College a Reality.* Retrieved February 25, 2008, from http://www.ihep.org/assets/files/publications/a-f/From_Aspiration_to_Action.pdf.

Data Quality Campaign. (n.d.). Retrieved November 3, 2008, from http://www.dataqualitycampaign.org/survey_results/elements.cfm#element9.

De Witt, J. C., Hansen, J. A., Rinkenberger, B. M. (2007). *2007–2008 State Report: Results of Indiana's Annual Career and College Information Survey of Students in Grades 9 and 11.* Retrieved September 18, 2008, from http://www.learnmoreindiana.org/SiteCollectionDocuments/2007-2008surveyreport.pdf

Dounay, J. (2007a). *Additional High School Graduation Requirements and Options.* Retrieved February 27, 2008, from http://mb2.ecs.org/reports/Report.aspx?id=740.

Dounay, J. (2007b). *Helping Equip Teachers to Answer Students' Questions on College Knowledge.* Retrieved February 28, 2008, from http://www.ecs.org/clearinghouse/73/72/7372.pdf.

Dounay, J. (2006). *Alignment of High School Graduation Requirements and State-Set College Admissions Requirements.* Retrieved February 27, 2008, from http://www.ecs.org/clearinghouse/68/60/6860.pdf.

Dynarski, S. M., & Scott-Clayton, J. E. (2006). Submitted for the National Tax Association Annual Conference: *The Feasibility of Delivering Aid for College Through the Tax System.*

Go Center Manual. (n.d.). Retrieved February 29, 2008, from http://techpreprgv.com/data/gocenters/Manualforschools.pdf.

Horatio Alger Association. (2005). *State of Our Nation's Youth 2005–2006.* Alexandria, Virginia: Author.

Hurst, D., Kelly, D., & Priciotta, D. (2005). Educational Attainment of High School Dropouts Eight Years Later. *Education Statistics Quarterly, volume 6* (issue 4). Retrieved February 27, 2008 from http://nces.ed.gov/programs/quarterly/vol_6/6_4/8_2.asp.

Indiana e-Transcript a. (n.d.). Retrieved February 28, 2008, from http://www.learnmoreindiana.org/college/applying/AdmissionsRequirements/Pages/IndianaETranscript.aspx.

Indiana e-Transcript b. (n.d.). Retrieved February 28, 2008, from http://www.learnmoreindiana.org/counselors/highschool/AcademicGuidance/Pages/Indiana_e-Transcript.aspx.

Indiana e-Transcript c. (n.d.). Retrieved February 28, 2008, from http://www.learnmoreindiana.org/counselors/highschool/AcademicGuidance/Pages/Indiana_e-Transcript.aspx#why.

Kirst, M., Venezia, A., & Antonio, A. L. (2004). What Have We Learned, and Where Do We Go Next? In Kirst, M.W., & Venezia, A. (Eds.), *From High School to College: Improving Opportunities for Success in Postsecondary Education* (pp. 285–319). San Francisco: Jossey-Bass.

Laird, J., DeBell, M., Kienzl, G., & Chapman, C. (2007). *Dropout Rates in the United States: 2005* (NCES 2007-059). U.S. Department of Education. Washington, DC: National Center for Education Statistics. Retrieved February 27, 2008 from http://nces.ed.gov/pubs2007/2007059.pdf.

Lake Snell Perry & Associates, Inc. (2003). *Leaks in the Postsecondary Pipeline: A Survey of Americans.* Retrieved February 22, 2008 from http://www.jff.org/Documents/LeakSurvey.pdf.

Markow, D., Liebman, M., & Dunbar, J., Sr. (2007). *Middle School Poll.* Retrieved February 26, 2008 from http://www.pdkintl.org/ms_poll/07ms_poll.pdf.

McDonough, P. M. (2005). Counseling Matters: Knowledge, Assistance, and Organizational Commitment in College Preparation. In W.G. Tierney, Z.B. Corwin, & J.E. Colyar (Eds.), *Preparing for College: Nine Elements of Effective Outreach* (pp. 69–87). Albany: State University of New York Press.

Merchant, B. (2004). Roadblocks to Effective K–16 Reform in Illinois. In Kirst, M.W., & Venezia, A. (Eds.), *From High School to College: Improving Opportunities for Success in Postsecondary Education* (pp. 115–150). San Francisco: Jossey-Bass.

Mintrop, H., Milton, T. H., Schmidtlein, F. A. & MacLellan, A. M. K–16 Reform in Maryland. In Kirst, M. W., & Venezia, A. (Eds.), *From High School to College: Improving Opportunities for Success in Postsecondary Education* (pp. 220–251). San Francisco: Jossey-Bass.

Mobile Go Center Makes Debut in Fort Worth to Help Close the Gap in College Participation. (2006a). Retrieved February 29, 2008, from http://www.att.com/gen/press-room?pid=4800&cdvn=news&newsarticleid=22888

Mobile Go Center to Help Close Education Gaps. (2006b). Retrieved February 29, 2008, from http://www.utsa.edu/today/2006/05/gocenter.cfm.

National Center for Higher Education Management Systems. (2002). "9th Graders Chance for College by Age 19." Retrieved February 26, 2008, from http://www.higheredinfo.org/dbrowser/index.php?measure=31.

National Center for Higher Education Management Systems and Jobs for the Future. (2007). *Adding It Up: State Challenges for Increasing College Access and Success.* Boston: Author.

National Postsecondary Education Cooperative. *Deciding on Postsecondary Education: Final Report* (NPEC 2008–850), prepared by Keith MacAllum, Denise M. Glover, Barbara Queen, and Angela Riggs. Washington, DC: 2007.

Ness, E. C. (2007). *Class of 2007 Senior Opinions Survey: Implications for College Access, College Choice, and the PROMISE Scholarship Program.* Retrieved February 26, 2008 from http://wvhepcdoc.wvnet.edu/resources/Class%20of%202007%20High%20School%20Senior%20Opinions%20Survey%20Attachment.pdf.

Public Agenda. (2006). Reality Check 2006, Issue No. 2: How Black and Hispanic Families Rate Their Schools. Retrieved February 22, 2008 from http://www.publicagenda.org/research/pdfs/rc0602.pdf.

Roderick, M., Nagaoka, J., Allensworth, E., Coca, V., Correa, M., & Stoker, G. (2006). From High School to the Future: A First Look at Chicago Public School Graduates' College Enrollment, College Preparation, and Graduation from Four-Year Colleges. Retrieved February 25, 2008 from http://ccsr.uchicago.edu/publications/Postsecondary.pdf.

Santiago, D. (2006). *California Policy Options to Accelerate Latino Success in Higher Education.* Retrieved February 27, 2008 from http://www.edexcelencia.org/pdf/FINAL-CAPolicyOptionsPRINT-11_27_06.pdf.

Social Science Research Council. (2005). *Questions That Matter: Setting the Research Agenda on Access and Success in Postsecondary Education.* New York: Author.

Tornatzky, L. G., Cutler, R., & Lee, J. (2002). *College Knowledge: What Latino Parents Need to Know and Why They Don't Know It.* Retrieved February 27, 2008 from http://www.trpi.org/PDFs/College_Knowledge.pdf.

2007–2008 Texas Common Application Freshman Admission. (2007). Retrieved February 29, 2008, from https://www.applytexas.org/adappc/thecb/Freshman07-08.pdf.

Turner, C. S. V., Jones, L. M., & Hearn, J. C. "Georgia's P–16 Reforms and the Promise of a Seamless System." In Kirst, M. W., & Venezia, A. (Eds.), *From High*

School to College: Improving Opportunities for Success in Postsecondary Education (pp. 183–219). San Francisco: Jossey-Bass.

Tyler, J. H. (2002). *The Economic Benefits of the GED: A Research Synthesis.* Retrieved February 27, 2008 from http://www.ncsall.net/fileadmin/resources/research/brief_tyler1.pdf.

U.S. Chamber of Commerce (2007). *Leaders and Laggards: A State-by-State Report Card on Educational Effectiveness.* Retrieved February 25, 2008 from www.uschamber.com/icw/reportcard.

Venezia, A. "K–16 Turmoil in Texas." In Kirst, M. W., & Venezia, A. (Eds.), *From High School to College: Improving Opportunities for Success in Postsecondary Education* (pp. 77–114). San Francisco: Jossey-Bass.

Venezia, A, & Kirst, M. "Inequitable Opportunities: How Current Education Systems and Policies Undermine the Chances for Student Persistence and Success in College." *Educational Policy,* 19 (2005), 283–307.

Venezia, A, Kirst, M., and Antonio, A., (2003). *Betraying the College Dream.* Retrieved February 28, 2008, from http://www.stanford.edu/group/bridgeproject/betrayingthecollegedream.pdf.

Welcome to the Mobile Go Center. (n.d.). Retrieved February 29, 2008, from http://www.austincc.edu/go/.

Yazzie-Mintz, E. (2007). *Voices of Students on Engagement: A Report on the 2006 High School Survey of Student Engagement.* Retrieved February 22, 2008 from http://ceep.indiana.edu/hssse/pdf/HSSSE_2006_Report.pdf.

Printed in the United States
218085BV00002B/2/P

9 781607 521242